WORD.
Savvy

nus (male) alumni (male) analysis analyses antenna antennae or antennas appe
endices or appendixes automaton automatons axis axes bacterium bacteria bas
u beaux or beaus bureau bureaus or bureaux cactus cacti or cactuses chateau
hateaus château châteaus or châteaux cherub cherubim or cherubs concerto co
certos corpus corpora cortex cortices or cortexes crisis crises criterion criteria c
icula or curriculums datum data diagnosis diagnoses dogma dogmas or dogma
ses emphasis emphases encyclopedia encyclopedias erratum errata focus focu
formula formulae or formulas forum forums or forma fungus fungi or funguses g
eaux genus genera hippopotamus hippopotamuses or hippopotami honorarium
onorariums hypothesis hypotheses index indices or indexes kibbutz kibbutzim la
is loci matrix matrices or matrixes matzo matzoth or matzos maximum maxima o
dium or media media (Media is now often treated as a singular mass noun.) me
norandums or memoranda millennium millenniums or millennia minimum minima
mums minutia minutiae mitzvah mitzvoth or mitzvahs nucleus nuclei or nucleuse
puses parenthesis parentheses persona personae or personas phenomenon p
eau plateaus or plateaux platypus platypuses radius radii or radiuses referendur
rendums schema schemata seraph seraphim or seraphs stadium stadia, stadiur
mata or stigmas stimulus stimuli stoma stomata or stomas stratum strata syllabu
yllabi symposium symposia or symposiums synopsis synopses synthesis synthe
eaux tableau tableaux or tableaus testis testes thesis theses trousseau trousse
sseaus trousseau trousseaux or trousseaus ultimatum ultimatums or ultimata ver
ebrae or vertebras vertex vertexes or vertices virus viruses vortex vortices or vor
elerated accentuated accomplished achieved acted activated actuated adapted
usted administered adopted advanced advertised advised advocated aided allo
lified analyzed answered anticipated applied appointed appraised approved ar
nged ascertained assembled assessed assigned assisted assumed attained au
mented authorized automated awarded balanced bargained began bolstered b
ght briefed broadened brought budgeted built calculated captured cataloged o
ified chaired championed charted checked clarified classified closed coached

WORD. Savvy

USE THE RIGHT WORD
EVERY TIME, ALL THE TIME

NANCY RAGNO

WRITER'S DIGEST
BOOKS

WritersDigest.*com*
Cincinnati, Ohio

For more resources for writers, visit www.writersdigest.com/books.

To receive a free weekly e-mail newsletter delivering tips and updates about writing and about Writer's Digest products, register directly at www.writersdigest.com/enews.

15 14 13 12 11   5 4 3 2 1

Distributed in Canada by Fraser Direct
100 Armstrong Avenue
Georgetown, Ontario, Canada L7G 5S4
Tel: (905) 877-4411

Distributed in the U.K and Europe by F&W Media International
Brunel House, Newton Abbot, Devon, TQ12 4PU, England
Tel: (+44) 1626-323200, Fax: (+44) 1626-323319
E-mail: postmaster@davidandcharles.co.uk

Distributed in Australia by Capricorn Link
P.O. Box 704, Windsor, NSW 2756 Australia
Tel: (02) 4577-3555

media

EDITED BY MELISSA WUSKE
DESIGNED BY TERRI WOESNER
PRODUCTION COORDINATED
BY DEBBIE THOMAS

Dedication

In memory of Sandra Ragno Murray, whose support and thoughtful suggestions were of great help to me while this book was still a work-in-progress.

Acknowledgments

To Melissa Wuske, my editor, for her invaluable help in shaping this book, her insightful editing, and her energy and never-failing enthusiasm, which made her a joy to work with.

To Kelly Messerly, Content Strategy Manager, for pointing me in the right direction for the book's focus and for having the faith to take it on and advocate its publication.

To Mike Myatt, Chief Strategy Officer, N2Growth, for permission to reprint an excerpt from "Buzzwords, They're not all bad" from his blog, N2Growth (www.n2growth.com/blog).

To Jim Murray for his helpful suggestions on quotations, memory tricks, and formatting for Chapter 3.

To the following websites, blogs, and their creators for providing instruction, motivation, and guidance on writing, communication skills, and social media.

Jo Barnes, founder, The Social Networking Academy: www.thesocialnetworkingacademy.com

Terry Whalin's blog, The Writing Life: http://terrywhalin.blogspot.com

Phyllis Zimbler Miller, social media strategist: www.millermosaicllc.com/book-marketing/

Joanna Penn's blog, The Creative Penn: www.thecreativepenn.com/

John Kremer, author and book marketing consultant: www.bookmarket.com

Jane Friedman's blog for Writer's Digest, There Are No Rules: http://blog.writersdigest.com/norules/

Contents

INTRODUCTION

This book gives you the tools you need to develop *word savvy,* an essential component of your success profile, one that can spell the difference between a lackluster, mediocre career and an outstanding one.

What exactly is word savvy? *Savvy* comes from the French *savoir faire:* "to be in the know; to have the ability to say or do the right thing." Word savvy enables you to choose the right word for the job—to say what you want to say or create the effect you aim to achieve. Word savvy prevents you from making wrong-word blunders—using *affect* when you mean *effect* or *compliment* when you mean *complement.* It prevents you from misusing words because you think you know what they mean, but you really don't. *Peruse,* for example, is commonly misused to mean "glance over quickly, to skim," whereas it really means "to examine thoroughly." Word savvy saves you from using nonwords, such as *irregardless,* or incorrect phrases, such as *couldn't care less.* It enables you to use tricky singular and plural forms with assurance—even when they come from foreign sources: e.g., *alumnus/alumni* and *alumna/alumnae.*

But that's not all. Being word savvy means that you keep abreast of the times. You stay on top of important new words entering the language and are alert for words you need to know. You are aware of the keywords computers are likely to scan for in your résumé. You know the important terms and current buzzwords in your field. Through word savvy you stay in the loop, maintain your competitive edge, and keep on top.

How can you achieve word savvy? This book tells you what you need to know. You'll learn how to:

- Master seventy-six commonly confused word pairs.

- Conquer fifty-two commonly misused words.
- Purge twenty-five no-no's from your speech and writing.
- Use tricky singulars and plurals with assurance.
- Include the right keywords in your résumé.
- Keep abreast of the new buzzwords in your field.

How is *Word Savvy* unique? First, it is comprehensive. Unlike other books, it presents six important components of word savvy: (1) commonly confused words; (2) commonly misused words; (3) popular no-no's—nonwords and illogical phrases; (4) tricky singulars and plurals; (5) buzzwords in the workplace; and (6) keywords for résumés. In addition, *Word Savvy* explains how wrong-word errors occur (sometimes due to no fault of the writer) and provides tips and techniques on how to spot wrong-word errors and proofread like a professional.

In addition to being comprehensive, *Word Savvy* is eminently practical. Its approach is honest, straightforward, and clear. It tells you what you want to know—information you need, information you will use. It deals with the word-choice problems you are most likely to encounter when you write. Although there are dozens of books available on word usage, most are not that practical. Typically, in order to include enough entries to fill a book, they are padded with esoteric and elitist terms—words that few would ever use, let alone confuse: e.g., *peccant* vs. *peccable, conterminous* vs. *contiguous,* and *emolument* vs. *emollient.*

Word Savvy is not for writers only. Being word savvy is a key to success in all areas of endeavor. Whether in business, science, the arts, academics, public service, or any other field or industry, the person who can use words clearly, accurately, effectively, and correctly is ahead of the game. Superior word savvy is not only admired but creates its own halo effect. That is, the person with superior word savvy is perceived to be superior in other areas as well—IQ, social skills, or job skills, for example. Thus, this book is a must for every success-oriented reader. *Word Savvy* is your key to success.

How This Book Is Organized

CHAPTERS 1 & 2 introduce the problem of wrong-word errors. Chapter 1 explains the extent of the problem, the kinds of words that are most likely to be confused, and why computerized spelling and editing programs can't be counted on to catch such errors. Chapter 2 explains why the usual methods of attacking the wrong-word problem don't work and presents two options for attacking the wrong-word problem systematically and effectively.

CHAPTER 3 consists of instructive entries for seventy-six pairs of commonly confused words. This chapter is designed for flexible use as both a wrong-word dictionary and a self-teaching text. Entries are alphabetized and cross-referenced, making the section ideal for use as a wrong-word dictionary. Each entry is self-teaching, self-testing, and self-correcting. Its aim is to help you *learn and remember* which word is which.

CHAPTER 4 is a quick reference guide to fifty-two commonly misused words. Information is presented in a table to make it quickly accessible. The listing for each word gives its mistaken meaning and its correct meaning.

CHAPTER 5 focuses on twenty-five no-no's to purge from your speech and writing. It covers both nonwords, such as *irregardless,* and incorrect phrases, such as *hone in on.* Information is presented in a quick-reference table.

CHAPTER 6 is a guide to tricky singular and plural forms. It deals with singulars and plurals of words "borrowed" from foreign languages; plurals of compound nouns; and plurals of proper names, numbers, and letters.

CHAPTER 7 reveals some surprising ways in which wrong-word errors can happen. It explains how such typos can occur even if you are adept at typing; how wrong-word errors can be initiated by spell-checkers; how use of a computerized thesaurus can cause you to choose a wrong word; and how word-usage errors can occur if you do not keep your audience in mind.

CHAPTER 8 emphasizes the importance of proofreading and provides proven tips and techniques on how to proofread like a professional.

CHAPTER 9 is both a departure and a bonus. Written with the success-oriented professional in mind, "Talk the Talk: Keeping Abreast of Buzzwords" discusses the effective use of buzzwords versus their widespread misuse, gives suggestions and resources for keeping on top of the latest buzzwords in your field, and—of vital concern to all job seekers—tells how to include the right keywords in your résumé to prepare your résumé for an electronic scan.

How to Use This Book

Word Savvy is designed for flexible use. It is both a handy reference guide and a self-teaching text. How you use the book is up to you. There is no set or predetermined order of its contents. Word entries are arranged alphabetically, a feature of the book which makes it ideal for use as a quick reference. Each pair of easily confused words has its own teaching plan that is designed to make it easy to understand how the words are different in meaning and usage. Lots of mnemonic devices, rhymes, hints, fascinating quotations, and informative examples help ensure that once you learn "which word is which," you won't forget it. A self-testing quiz ends each teaching plan. It enables you to see if you understand and can use what you just learned or if you should go back and review the material. Quizzes are nonthreatening. Their subject matter is informative, fun, or both.

Dip into *Word Savvy* as you choose. Use it as a quick reference guide to commonly confused words. Use it as a self-teaching text on how to choose the right word, conquer words that are commonly misused, purge no-no's from your vocabulary, use tricky singulars and plurals, keep abreast of buzzwords in your field, and include the right buzzwords in your résumé.

Word Savvy is an indispensable writer's companion, a comprehensive guide on how to avoid embarrassing and costly wrong-word errors and use the right word every time, all the time. Keep your copy handy, next to your computer, ready to consult whenever you compose an e-mail, business letter, term paper, blockbuster novel, or sonnet—whatever it is you wish to communicate with the written world. Success starts with *Word Savvy.*

01

AVOID THE NO. 1 MISTAKE OF TODAY'S WRITERS

> *Critics search for ages for the wrong word, which, to give them credit, they eventually find.*
>
> —PETER USTINOV

What is the most common error made by today's writers? According to a mammoth nationwide study conducted by Stanford University in 2005–2006, the No. 1 error is now *choosing the wrong word*. Wrong-word errors account for almost 14 percent of the top twenty most common errors in writing. This is dramatic news. Now, for the first time, wrong-word errors top spelling errors—and by a substantial margin. The Stanford study was conducted by Andrea A. and Karen Lunsford to update the *St. Martin's Handbook's* groundbreaking 1986 research on the most common writing errors of college students. In 1986, spelling errors outnumbered all other common errors in writing three to one. In 2006, they accounted for only 6.5 percent of those errors—a dramatic decline. (Thanks, spell-checker!)

Wrong-word errors are not only common, they are embarrassing and costly. They can sink your credibility with your reader. and make you appear ignorant. That is the bad news. But take heart. There is good news. It is not that hard to learn to recognize and correct the problem. The overwhelming majority of wrong-word errors fall into the "words commonly confused" category—pairs and even trios of words that almost everyone confuses at some time or another because they sound alike or have similar spellings or somewhat related meanings. What does it take to correct such common wrong-word errors? It takes some self-instruction and study. You need to sensitize yourself to words that cause problems so you can quickly spot them in your own writing. And you need to learn their meanings and usage—how the words in the frequently confused word pair differ from each other.

Where can you find the information you need to combat wrong-word errors? You'll find it in Chapter 2, "Attacking the Wrong-Word Problem," and Chapter 3, "Master 76 Commonly Confused Word Pairs." The small investment of time you spend mastering the most commonly confused words will repay itself many times over. Being word savvy in this important area means you can be confident that you will avoid common word blunders and use the right word every time.

HOMONYMS: CONFUSION REIGNS (RAINS? REINS?)

English has a larger, richer vocabulary than any other language in the world. Ironically, this apparent boon to writers presents a problem. With so many words, so many choices, it is all too easy to mistakenly choose the wrong word and introduce an error into your writing. Such unintentional slips of the pen not only confuse the reader but may embarrass the writer, as well. English has an abundance of words that are easily confused. Among the most confusing are *homonyms* (also called *homophones*). Homonyms are words that sound alike but have different spellings and meanings. Homonyms are high on the list of words most frequently confused by English-speaking peoples from grade three through adulthood. They include such commonly used words as: *to/too/two ... hear/here ... there/ their/they're ... principal/principle ... capital/capitol ... complement/compliment ... coarse/course ...* and *sight/cite/site.*

Homonyms are not a problem in spoken English because there is no audible difference between them. Spelling is not an issue. In written English, however, it is a different matter. Writing the wrong homonym can make of muddle of meaning. Consider the confusion that could result by writing *maul* instead of *mall, foul* instead of *fowl, chaste* instead of *chased,* or *bare* instead of *bear,* for example. Not only does the wrong word create confusion on the part of the reader, but once recognized, it can lower the reader's esteem for the writer and devalue what the writer is trying to say.

Before leaving homonyms, however, it should be noted that choosing the wrong one may be an intentional choice—especially if the writer is a punster. Homonyms provide a wealth of opportunities to spark up writing with puns, wordplay, and double entendre by enabling the writer to say one thing and imply another.

THOSE PROBLEMATIC PRONOUNS

POSSESSIVE FORMS. When choosing between two pronouns, it is all too easy to choose the wrong one. Two characteristics of pronouns are responsible for this propensity to confuse. First, unlike nouns, pronouns have special forms to show possession. Nouns show possession by adding an apostrophe *s* or, for words that already end in *s*, an apostrophe. In contrast, pronouns use special forms to show possession. Those forms are shown below.

PERSONAL PRONOUNS	SINGULAR	PLURAL
1st person	my, mine	our, ours
2nd person	your, yours	your, yours
3rd person	his, her, hers, its	their, theirs
Relative pronoun	whose	whose

Notice that none of those forms include an apostrophe. Pronouns do add apostrophes for another reason, however. Therein lies the confusion. Whereas nouns add apostrophes to show possession, pronouns add apostrophes to form contractions.

It is easy to see how this ambiguous use of the apostrophe could cause confusion. And it does. Remembering subconsciously that an apostrophe shows possession, writers mistakenly write *it's, you're,* and *they're* when what they really mean is *its, your,* and *their.*

CASE. The second problem with pronouns is that they have "case." That is, they have different forms to show how they are used in a sentence—whether they are used as a subject or an object, for example. This is a hangover from earlier times centuries ago when English was a highly inflected language that depended on word forms and inflected endings to show the function of a word in a sentence. When English adopted "natural word order," the position of a word in the sentence indicated its function. Inflected endings and differing word forms were no longer necessary, and most gradually dropped off or disappeared—that is, except for pronouns. Pronouns retained their differing forms to indicate their function in the sentence. They retained their case.

The fact that pronouns have case gives English yet another opportunity to confuse its users. Having to choose between the subject or object form of a pronoun provides boundless opportunities to choose the wrong one. For example, which is the correct choice for each of these: (1) "It is me" or "It is I"; (2) "between you and me" or "between you and I"; (3) "with him and me" or "with him and I"? (See page 186, Answers.)

The following table shows the case forms of pronouns: i.e., *subject pronouns* and *object pronouns*. In grammar books, subject pronouns are said to be in the *nominative case* and object pronouns in the *objective case*. (Those terms were adopted from Latin grammar and are not particularly useful to describe the grammar of English.) Table 3 shows when to use subject pronouns and when to use object pronouns.

PERSONAL PRONOUNS	SUBJECT PRONOUNS		OBJECT PRONOUNS	
	Singular	Plural	Singular	Plural
1st person	I	we	me	us
2nd person	you	you	you	you
3rd person	he, she, it	they	him, her, it	them
Relative pronoun	who	who	whom	whom

USING SUBJECT PRONOUNS

1. Use a subject pronoun as a subject of a verb.
   We climbed Mt. Kilimanjaro.
   He and *I* jogged around the lake.
   Who fired that shot?

2. Use a subject pronoun as a predicate nominative (i.e., after a linking verb).
   It is *I*.
   It was *she* who laughed last.
   It was *they* who won the World Series.

USING OBJECT PRONOUNS

1. Use an object pronoun as the direct object of a verb.
   We chose *her* as leader.
   The rain pelted *us*.
   The dog approached *me* cautiously.

2. Use an object pronoun as the indirect object of a verb.
   They gave *us* a ride.
   Did he give *her* the correct change?
   Please leave *me* a message.

3. Use an object pronoun as the object of a preposition.
   Did you give the briefcase to *her*?
   Let's keep this between *you* and *me*.
   Jeff's brother will ride with *him* and *me*.

LEVELS OF USAGE. Complicating the problem of choosing the right pronoun is the fact that English is not static. It is a living language, and its usage rules are not cast in concrete. Changes in usage move from the spoken language (where they become generally accepted) to the written language (where they are accepted first in informal writing only). Formal written English is slow to change. It is the last bastion of correct English, the habitat of grammarians, English teachers, academicians, and all those who pride themselves on the correctness (hence superiority) of their grammar.

Sometimes it is not enough to know what the correct word is. Writers and speakers may need to consider their intended audience. English has various levels of usage, and the correct word choice may not always be the best word choice, as the following joke shows:

> Knock , knock.
> *Who's there?*
> It is I.
> *It's that *#@cx%+# English teacher again!*

THOSE VEXING VERBS

Ironically the verbs that vex the most are those among the most useful, common, and frequently used. The following pairs of commonly confused verbs cause confusion because their formal "correct" usage is often at odds with their everyday use in spoken English: *can/may, bring/ take, shall/will, was/were, lay/lie, set/sit.* Because English is continually changing (and because of the continued misuse of those verbs in conversation and the media), distinctions between them are gradually disappearing. In fact, the correct usage may sound stilted or bookish. The bad news is that it is still necessary to know and observe the rules in formal written English, especially when you are striving to make the best possible impression on your reader and that reader may be unfavorably influenced by any lapse of correct grammar on your part.

WORDS LINKED BY MEANING

It is easy to confuse words that are used in a similar context and have related meanings—such words as: *imply/infer, prone/supine, libel/slander, acute/ chronic, aggravate/irritate, compare/contrast, connote/denote, emigrate/im- migrate, empathy/sympathy, fewer/less.* Fortunately most of us recognize our confusion when we are about to use one of those words: "Do I mean *imply* or *infer?*" "Should I sue for *libel* or for *slander?*" "Is my cough *acute* or *chronic?*" Recognizing your confusion is the first step in clearing it up.

Surprisingly it is not always possible to clear up such confusion by observing how public figures—even famous writers—use such words. For an example of this, try finding a quote that illustrates the correct usage of *emigrate* as compared to *immigrate*. You will find this to be a most frustrating assignment. Does this mean that the general public is grammatically challenged, unaware that one *emigrates from* and *immigrates to* and similar distinctions? Not at all. It does mean, however, that English is a living language, continually (not *continuously*) changing, and that perhaps one repeats what one hears most often.

WORDS LINKED BY SOUND

Homonyms are confused because they sound alike. Words that sound somewhat or almost alike are confused, as well. When two words have a similar sound, it is easy to substitute one for another and write a perfectly spelled word that is the wrong word. This explains the common confusion between such similarly sounding words as these: *accept/except, affect/effect, assure/ensure/insure, elicit/illicit, flaunt/flout,* and *weather/whether.*

As with homonyms, words linked by sound can inject humor into writing—intentional or otherwise. Mrs. Malaprop, a character in the 1775 comedy *The Rivals,* by Richard Brinsley Sheridan, was famous for such incorrect word choices. She inspired the term "malapropism" (the incorrect use of a word caused by confusion over a similar sound or spelling). Mrs. Malaprop, true to her name, strides through the play dropping malapropisms. Here are a few of her originals:

- She's as headstrong as an *allegory* on the Nile. (*alligator*)
- He is the very *pineapple* of politeness. (*pinnacle*)
- I have laid Sir Anthony's *preposition* before her. (*proposition*)
- I hope you will represent her to the captain as an object not altogether *illegible*. (*eligible*)
- Why, murder's the matter! slaughter's the matter! killing's the matter!—but he can give you the *perpendiculars*. (*particulars*)

- Sure, if I *reprehend* anything in this world it is the use of my *oracular* tongue, and a nice *derangement* of *epitaphs!* (*apprehend, vernacular, arrangement, epithets*)

Malapropisms did not end with the eighteenth-century character Mrs. Malaprop. Here are a few contemporary malapropisms from miscellaneous sources:

- I'm dropping our goalkeeper. He's too *erotic.* (*erratic*)
- I got stuck in the *revolting* doors. (*revolving*)
- Their father was some kind of civil *serpent.* (*servant*)
- A rolling stone gathers no *moths.* (*moss*)
- Flying saucers are just an optical *conclusion.* (*illusion*)

A MIXED BLESSING

The fabulously rich vocabulary of English gives you an enormous advantage over writers in other languages. It multiplies your chances of finding the right words to express exactly what you mean. But the huge vocabulary of English is a mixed blessing. Multiplying word choices also multiples opportunities for confusion. As a writer, you need to make yourself aware of the kinds of words that are most likely to trip you up. Familiarize yourself with the most commonly confused words. Learn and remember their correct usages and meanings. And ... beware of the kinds of words most likely to snare the unwary writer—homonyms, possessive pronouns, and commonly misused verbs. Finally, be vigilant. Be suspicious, not complacent, lest you commit a malapropism or absentmindedly write the wrong word of an easily confused pair.

02

Attacking the Wrong-Word Problem

Create a definite plan for carrying out your desire and begin at once, whether you're ready or not, to put the plan into action.

—Napoleon Hill

This is the age of the computer. Why be concerned about choosing the right homonym or pronoun, or of figuring out which word is which? Why not just leave the task to your spell-checker and grammar-checker tools? Word checking seems to be the sort of task ideally suited to a computer. Plus, there's always the dictionary. Many excellent dictionaries are accessible online at the click of a mouse.

If only it were that easy! In regard to depending on your computer to catch your errors, perhaps Adam Osborne said it best: "People think computers will keep them from making mistakes. They're wrong. With computers you make mistakes faster."

WHAT YOUR SPELL-CHECKER WON'T TELL YOU

A spell-checker is superb at doing what it was designed to do—alert you to misspelled words and suggest corrections. What a spell-checker won't do, however, is alert you to a perfectly spelled word that is the wrong word. Spell-checkers are not designed to pay attention to word meanings. Even if the wrong word is the result of a typo, it won't fall under a spell-checker's scrutiny if it is spelled correctly.

Although spell-checkers catch spelling errors, they can cause wrong-word errors, according to Professor Andrea A. Lunsford of Stanford University:

> But every blessing brings its own curse. In this case, many of the wrong-word errors appear to be the result of spell-checker suggestions. A student trying to spell "frantic," for example, apparently accepted the spell-checker's suggestion of "fanatic." Wrong word for sure.

WHAT YOUR GRAMMAR CHECKER WON'T TELL YOU

Grammar checkers claim that they spot mistakes in word usage. They do—sometimes. That is the problem. Grammar checkers are inconsistent. They may catch a misused word one time and completely miss the same error another time. A second problem with grammar checkers is that even when they point out a "wrong word," you still need to check it by looking up the word and its alternates and then deciding on the correct word choice. Another problem with grammar checkers is that the "possible wrong words" they do catch are often correct. You need to be wary of being intimidated by grammar-checker queries and changing a right word to a wrong word.

The following sentences illustrate the folly of relying on a grammar checker to catch all word-choice errors. The passage was checked by a widely used grammar-check program. It contains twelve word-choice blunders. How many did the grammar-checker catch? None. (See the corrected paragraph on page 186.)

> If you're thinking you can rely on a spell-checker or grammar-check program too error-proof you're manuscript or even to site your principle or every day errors in usage, let me insure you, your sadly mistaken. You need to quantify that belief or leave it go. Will such programs tell you, i.e., weather to use *I* or *me* after the proposition *with*?

WHAT ABOUT DICTIONARIES?

Dictionaries are the ultimate authorities on word meaning and usage. There are even wrong-word dictionaries and dictionaries of commonly confused words that can be accessed online. So why not look up any suspect word in a dictionary? A dictionary is the key to choosing the right word every time. Right? Not entirely.

Here is the dilemma. A dictionary is only helpful *if* you consult it. But *will* you consult it? Not unless you suspect that a word you wrote—or are about to write—is the wrong word. How can you overcome this dilemma?

TRAIN YOUR INNER EDITOR

Armed with your computerized editing programs and dictionary, it would seem that you are well prepared for any wrong-word encounter. To a certain extent, you are. This doesn't mean, however, that you can type on with reckless abandon, confident that you are safe from making a word blunder. Remember, grammar checkers don't catch all errors. Along with spell-checkers, they can even lure you into replacing a right word with a wrong one. Dictionaries provide solutions to word-choice problems, but they don't diagnose them. By all means, use computerized editing programs to check your writing every time you write for someone else's eyes. If you find a problem word, look it up. But be aware that in this age of computer-assisted writing, the world's best editor is still the one that resides in your head. You must be able to trust your inner editor. Therefore, train your inner editor. Train it—and use it.

You can train yourself to be a better editor. You can become proficient at avoiding, spotting, and correcting wrong-word problems. The first step is to familiarize yourself with the words that are most likely to cause problems—the words most commonly confused. The dictionary of commonly confused words that makes up chapter 3 is ideal for doing this.

METHODS OF ATTACK

You may prefer to look up and study the entries in chapter 3 on a need-to-know basis, as questions about "which word is which" crop up in your writing. Or you may prefer to develop a plan to study the word entries systematically. The organization of each entry is explained in chapter 3, page 21. Below are suggestions for developing a systematic plan for studying the entries.

Option 1. Begin with the words most likely to cause you trouble.

1. Scan the listings for 76 Commonly Confused Word Pairs that begin on page 22. Your object is to check off word pairs that cause you no problem. You are confident in using them and know how they differ in meaning and usage.

2. Before mentally crossing off an entry, do a quick check to make sure you really do know how the words differ. Mentally fill in the words (or write in the book) for the quiz sentences at the end of the entry and check your answers at the back of the book. This will tell you whether or not you need to work through that entry. Your score should be 100 percent correct.

3. After you have eliminated words you're sure you know how to use, study the remaining words systematically, as suggested below.

Option 2. Begin with the first entry, "accept, except."

1. Set a goal for yourself. For example, aim to learn a pair of words a day or a certain number a week. Then tackle the entries in order.

2. Suppose you have decided to tackle two word entries a day. Master those words; then move on.

3. A week later, go back and retest yourself on the quizzes for the entries you learned the week before. Review as needed.

USE THE QUIZZES

The organization of an entry is explained on pages 21–22. A self-quiz ends each entry. A word of advice: However tempting it may be, don't skip the quizzes. Just as reading is a passive activity when compared to writing, "book learning" is not as dynamic or as permanent as learning by doing. As one of our Founding Fathers, Benjamin Franklin, put it, "Tell me and I forget. Teach me and I remember. Involve me and I learn."

The quizzes that end each entry are meant to do just that—involve you so that you learn. The quizzes are important for two reasons. They show you what you have learned or still need to learn. They also provide practice in making the same word choices you will be faced with when you write, thus helping you avoid real-time mistakes as a writer.

USE ALL YOUR SENSES

Educational psychologists tell us that the best way to learn something is to incorporate as many senses as possible in the process of learning. The act of reading, for example, utilizes the sense of *sight* (or *touch* if you're reading Braille). Reading aloud adds the senses of *hearing* and *touch* to the sense of sight. Obviously, you hear what you read aloud, but how is the sense of touch involved? When you form the words in you mouth and speak, you use muscles. Moving your muscles triggers the sense of feeling, or touch. Is there a way to incorporate the sense of smell into learning? Possibly. (If you can figure out a way to do this, your fortune is made!) The point is that using multiple senses to learn something enhances learning.

How can this concept be allied to learning how to distinguish between commonly confused words? Reading aloud the completed quiz sentences at the end of the book is a good start. Read them aloud repeatedly until they "sound right." Not only will you be using three senses to learn—you will be learning correct usage through repetition.

It is hard to remember correct word usage if it does not "sound right." There are several reasons the correct usage may sound awkward.

Perhaps most people use the word incorrectly when they speak. We become accustomed to hearing the incorrect usage. It sounds right to us. Or, the word's generally accepted usage might be in the process of changing. As the incorrect usage is heard more and more frequently, it eventually becomes accepted. At that point the old correct usage doesn't sound right.

Those who are learning English as a second language have a special problem. The spoken English they hear differs in some respects from the English taught in English textbooks. For all these reasons it is necessary to become acquainted with correct usage. One of the best ways to do this is to repeat correct usage aloud until it sounds right.

BECOME A WORD CRITIC

Don't stop with the word entries in this book. Go beyond. Pay attention to what you read and what you hear. Notice how other people are using the language. No doubt you will be surprised at how often the rules are being broken, even by the most noted speakers and writers. Even they are not immune from occasionally making a wrong-word error.

Paying attention to how other people use the language will sharpen your linguistic sensitivity and prompt you to pay closer attention to your own use of words. In your role as word critic, be flexible. Keep in mind that English is not a static language but changes gradually to reflect how people are using it. Another principle to keep in mind is that the grammars of spoken and written English are not identical. Spoken English, for example, is characterized by sentence fragments, uncomplicated sentence structure, repetitions, redundancies, informal vocabulary, and contractions. All of these departures from the traditions of formal written English contribute to the effectiveness and vibrancy of spoken English. If they were transcribed into formal written English, however, the result would be confusion, lack of focus, and a failure to communicate. If the medium is the message, then let the message fit the medium.

In conclusion, keep your eyes and ears open to how the language is changing, how the rules of formal written English are being bent and broken. Become a word critic, but at the same time know correct formal written English usage and become adept in using it. Remember that at many important junctures of your life, you will be judged by what you write. At those times in particular it is crucial that you use the right words.

03
MASTER 76 COMMONLY CONFUSED WORD PAIRS

*The difference between the right word and the almost right word
is the difference between lightning and a lightning bug.*

—MARK TWAIN

This chapter is designed to enable you to learn and remember
which word is which when choosing between a troublesome pair, such
as *who's* or *whose, accept* or *except, libel* or *slander.* Entries are listed in
alphabetical order and are cross-indexed. This organization enables you
to use the chapter for a variety of purposes, depending on your needs:

- Use it as a *wrong-word dictionary*—a quick reference guide to
  consult whenever you suspect that the word you wrote—or are
  about to write—is the wrong word.

- Use it to check on a *word's meaning* and for *examples of correct
  usage.* Each entry includes definitions and parts of speech as
  well as example sentences and quotations.

- Use it as a *self-teaching text* to:
    - familiarize yourself with words that are frequently confused
      so you can be on the lookout for them.
    - understand what each word means and how it is used.
    - recognize the distinctions between easily confused words.
    - develop memory tricks and mnemonic devices to help you
      remember the distinctions between the words.

• test yourself on your ability to apply what you've learned.

HOW A WORD ENTRY IS ORGANIZED

The entry for each pair of commonly confused words is set up like this: (1) quotations, (2) definitions, (3) example sentences, (4) usage notes, (5) memory tricks, and (6) a quiz. The different parts of an entry are explained below and are labeled on the sample entry for loose, lose shown on page 99.

1. QUOTES. Each entry opens with quotes that illustrate usage of the entry words by well-known public figures. Authors of the quotes encompass a wide range of personages—from Mae West to Winston Churchill—chosen to illustrate correct usage, yet interesting enough to be read for pure enjoyment.

2. DEFINITIONS. Dictionary definitions of the words in question follow the example quotes. Some words have a number of definitions. Not all of them are listed. The most commonly used meanings are, however, along with the word's part of speech.

3. EXAMPLE SENTENCES. These sentences illustrate the use of each word for the various meanings given. An example sentence is given for each of the primary meanings of the word.

4. USAGE NOTES. Sometimes a word's definition needs to be expanded to explain a common problem or an exception to its usage. Usage notes call attention to these issues and alert you to common mistakes in usage.

5. MEMORY TRICKS. Being able to recognize that the word you are about to write may not be the word you mean is the first step to choosing the right word. But how can you remember which word is which? It helps to use memory tricks. Probably the best aids to memory are those you invent yourself. To assist you, however, each entry supplies a few memory boosters: mnemonic devices, rhymes, alliterative sentences, connections with related words and spellings, and suggested visualizations.

6. **QUIZ.** The lesson ends with a self-test to help you see whether or not you understand the material and will apply it when you write. Answers are at the back of the book. Although the entries provide considerable information to explain "which word is which," providing information is not always enough. Most of us have had the experience of reading an explanation and thinking we understand it—until we try to apply it. As the saying goes, "The proof is in the pudding." The real test comes when you sit down to write. Will you be on the alert for commonly confused words and remember the distinctions between them? Self-testing helps you see what you've learned versus what you only thought you learned.

accept, except

You have to accept whatever comes, and the only important thing is that you meet it with courage and with the best you have to give.
—ELEANOR ROOSEVELT

Once we accept our limits, we go beyond them.
—ALBERT EINSTEIN

A life is not important except for its impact on other lives.
—JACKIE ROBINSON

Everything has been figured out, except how to live.
—JEAN-PAUL SARTRE

ACCEPT *v.* 1. To receive willingly. 2. To agree with; to put up with.

EXCEPT *prep.* With the exception of; not including. *v.* To exclude; to take out from the rest.

> I am pleased to *accept* this award.
>
> I *accept* the conclusions of your report.
>
> Everyone was wrong *except* Harry.
>
> If you *except* weather delays, arrivals were on time.

(T) MEMORY TRICKS

- **CONNECT:** *accept → acceptance.*
- **VISUALIZE & ALLITERATION:** Visualize yourself bowing to thunderous applause after playing an accordion solo. Think, "I gladly *accept* your *acclaim* and *accolades* for my *accomplishments* on the *accordion.*"
- **CONNECT:** *except → exception → exceptional.*
- **VISUALIZE & CONNECT:** Visualize yourself beaming and wearing the banner *Exceptional!*" Think, "*Except* for one rare *exception*, I am *exceptional!*"

(Q) QUIZ   answers on page 186

1. It's logical to expect that an Oscar-caliber actor would not _____ a role in a ridiculously bad movie _____ under dire circumstances.

2. Thus, _____ for die-hard John Wayne fans, few movie goers could _____ Wayne in the incongruous role of Genghis Khan in *The Conqueror.*

3. Critics did not _____ director Dick Powell from responsibility for the absurd Asian Western, whose star would _____ an Oscar thirteen years later for his role as a one-eyed U.S. marshal in *True Grit.*

4. Evidently Powell was willing to _____ Wayne's statement that he saw *The Conqueror* as a cowboy film and would play Khan as a gunslinger, _____ that he slung a sword.

5. _____ for transporting the Gobi Desert to Utah, _____ for the preposterous casting of the Duke as Genghis Khan and Susan Hayward as a Tartar princess, viewers might have been willing to _____ the premise of the film.

acute, chronic

I find the pain of a little censure, even when it is unfounded, is more acute than the pleasure of much praise.
—THOMAS JEFFERSON

The shock of any trauma, I think, changes your life. It's more acute in the beginning and after a little time you settle back to what you were. However it leaves an indelible mark on your psyche.

—ALEX LIFESON

Every citizen who stops smoking, or loses a few pounds, or starts managing his chronic disease with real diligence, is caulking a crack for the benefit of us all.

—MITCH DANIELS

Nothing irritates me more than chronic laziness in others. Mind you, it's only mental sloth I object to. Physical sloth can be heavenly.

—ELIZABETH HURLEY

ACUTE *adj.* 1. Sharp; shrewd; penetrating. 2. (*Medicine*) reaching a crisis rapidly and having a short course (as of a disease).

CHRONIC *adj.* Of long duration; constant.

>She has an *acute* and biting wit and always has a ready retort.
>
>He experienced *acute* stomach pain that lasted ten minutes.
>
>Unfortunately, pain-relieving medications are only a temporary relief for *chronic* back pain.
>
>He is, and no doubt will always be, a *chronic* complainer.

 MEMORY TRICKS

- **CONNECT:** *acute* → *cut*. (*Acute* contains the smaller word *cut*. A cut is made by something sharp.)
- **CONNECT:** *acute* → *accident* (a critical medical emergency).
- **CONNECT:** *chronic* → *chronology*. (Both are concerned with a stretch of time. A *chronic* disease is long term. A *chronology* arranges events in a time sequence.)

QUIZ   answers on page 186

1. Can a virus cause _____ fatigue syndrome?
2. Your _____ lateness will get you fired!
3. She was hospitalized with _____ appendicitis.

4. Gifted with _____ intelligence, the chimp easily won the game of checkers from his partner, whose _____ hyperactivity always interfered with her ability to concentrate.

5. A broken arm is an example of a medical condition that is _____, whereas asthma is a condition that is _____.

advice, advise

In giving advice, seek to help, not to please, your friend.

—DIOGENES

No enemy is worse than bad advice.

—SOPHOCLES

We are so happy to advise others that occasionally we even do it in their interest.

—JULES RENARD

I have found the best way to give advice to your children is to find out what they want and then advise them to do it.

—HARRY S. TRUMAN

ADVICE *n.* Recommendation; suggestion; counsel; guidance.

ADVISE *v.* 1. To recommend; give advice to. 2. To inform.

My *advice* is to follow your dream.

Do you want *advice* on how to succeed?

I *advise* reading Napoleon Hill's book *Think and Grow Rich*.

Please *advise* your clients about the new tax laws.

(T) MEMORY TRICKS

- **RHYME:** *Advice* can be *nice*, like sugar and *spice*, or can lead you to *vice*, such as gambling with *dice*.
- **RHYME:** Always think *twice* before taking *advice*.
- **RHYME:** Since you are so *wise*, then please *advise*; should I stick to my guns or *compromise*?
- **RHYME:** Some *advise* you to *exercise* before you eat when you first *arise*.

QUIZ   answers on page 187

1. Do you need an expert to _____ you on how to solve your problem?
2. The following paragraphs give some useful _____.
3. Much _____ is available on what to do when your dog has a skunk encounter—some helpful, some not.
4. The _____ given by most dog owners is to saturate your pet in tomato juice; but others _____ using vinegar.
5. Both pieces of _____ simply distract the nose without curing the problem.
6. What do veterinarians _____?
7. Their _____ is to mix the following in an open container: 1 quart of 3 percent hydrogen peroxide, ¼-cup baking soda, and 1 to 2 teaspoons of mild dishwashing detergent that does not contain ammonia or bleach.
8. They _____ saturating your pet's coat with the mixture and letting it set five minutes before rinsing.
9. One last piece of _____ is to avoid keeping the mixture in a closed container because it can explode.

advise *See* advice

affect, effect

The consequences of an act affect the probability of its occurring again.
    —B.F. SKINNER

Chocolate causes certain endocrine glands to secrete hormones that affect your feelings and behavior by making you happy.
    —ELAINE SHERMAN

The best effect of fine persons is felt after we have left their presence.
    —RALPH WALDO EMERSON

When did we begin to lose faith in our ability to effect change?
    —WYNTON MARSALIS

AFFECT *v.* 1. To influence; have an effect on. 2. To pretend; feign. 3. *n.* (in psychology) Feeling; emotion.

EFFECT *n.* A result; consequence. *v.* To bring about; cause to pass.

> The drought will *affect* farmers adversely.
>
> She likes to *affect* a British accent.
>
> The subject's reaction and *affect* were normal.
>
> One *effect* of the drought is increased food prices.
>
> It is hoped that the new drug will *effect* a cure.

T · MEMORY TRICKS

- **ALPHABETICAL & LOGICAL ORDER:** When you **affect** something you produce an **effect** on it.

- **VISUALIZATION & ALLITERATION:** Visualize yourself contemplating an attractive stranger who is covered with ten-dollar bills. Think, "How will this **affair affect** my **aff**luence, and can I **aff**ord it?"

- **CONNECT:** *cause → effect.*

Q · QUIZ   answers on page 187

1. We are all familiar with the _____ of biting into a red-hot chili pepper.

2. We may _____ indifference, but our taste buds _____ a protest to the fiery hot _____ of capsaicin, the ingredient that causes red hots to _____ us with their built in fire.

3. But that fiery _____ may _____ us in beneficial ways.

4. New studies point to capsaicin's detrimental _____ on cancer cells.

5. For malignant cells, capsaicin can _____ a premature death.

6. Capsaicin's fiery _____ is put to use in a barnacle repellant applied to boats.

7. Capsaicin can _____ and dull the perception of pain, an anesthetic _____.

8. The sting of capsaicin can _____ a release of endorphins.

9. This creates the _____ of a mild high—which explains why pepper lovers keep coming back for more, in spite of the fire.

aggravate, irritate

In desperate straits, the fears of the timid aggravate the dangers that imperil the brave.

—CHRISTIAN NEVELL BOVEE

Since grief only aggravates your loss, grieve not for what is past.

—WALKER PERCY

A sure means to irritate people and to put evil thoughts into their heads is to keep them waiting a long time.

—FRIEDRICH NIETZSCHE

Look at that married woman—sleepless nights and toilsome days cloud her brow and irritate her temper.

—HARRIOT K. HUNT

AGGRAVATE *v.* To make worse; intensify.

IRRITATE *v.* 1. To annoy; exasperate. 2. To inflame.

> Pollutants can *aggravate* allergy symptoms.
>
> Bruce likes to *irritate* his little brother.
>
> Some strong detergents can *irritate* the skin. (inflame)

Ⓣ MEMORY TRICKS

- **CONTRAST:** People are not *aggravated* or *aggravating*; things are *aggravating*. People are *irritated* or *irritating*. (Note: This distinction is often ignored in informal usage.)
- **CONNECT:** *aggravate → aggravated assault.*
- **ALLITERATION:** Think, "*Irritating Irving irks* me" (to connect *irritate* with a person).

Ⓠ QUIZ   answers on page 187

1. Did Jean's remarks _____ John?
2. Did John's temper tantrum _____ a bad situation?
3. Poison ivy can _____ the skin.
4. Can unusual stress _____ acne?

5. Neglect of agriculture can _____ poverty.

all ready, already

I'm all ready you see. Now my troubles are going to have trouble with me!
—THEODOR SEUSS GEISEL (DR. SEUSS)

We're all ready to play and get out there and get it done.
—DUSTIE ROBERTSON

There cannot be a crisis today; my schedule is already full.
—HENRY KISSINGER

Unless you try to do something beyond what you have already mastered, you will never grow.
—RALPH WALDO EMERSON

ALL READY *adj.* Completely ready; prepared.

ALREADY *adv.* Prior to; previously; beforehand.

> My bags are packed; I'm *all ready* to go.
> I've *already* packed my bags; I'm ready to go.

MEMORY TRICKS

- **LISTEN:** Mentally say the sentence you are about to write. If you pause between *all* and *ready*, use two words, **all ready**.
- **VISUALIZE & CONNECT:** Visualize runners ready to start a race. Think, "**All ready?** All set? Go!"
- **VISUALIZE & CONNECT:** Visualize yourself waiting for a friend and looking at your watch, distressed. Think, "It's __almost__ 8:00 and we're __already__ late!"

QUIZ   answers on page 187

1. Are you _____ for the big one—an event bigger than the predicted big earthquake in California?

2. This is something that _____ occurred once before, some 65 million years ago, when the Earth was _____ into the Age of Dinosaurs.

3. An asteroid collided with Earth, producing a dust cloud and resulting cold temperatures that killed thousands of species—and, we are _____ overdue for another such collision.

4. Preparations have _____ started to ensure we will be _____ to prevent our extinction when the next one arrives.

5. _____, we are scanning the skies for approaching asteroids, and _____ we are making plans to divert them with missiles or whatever it takes.

6. Preparations are _____ being made to avoid a collision so that we will be _____ to defend ourselves if it becomes necessary.

all ready *See* already

all together, altogether

For years, I've pushed the idea of a column compilation book mainly because it would be easy—I could just staple 'em all together.
—MICHAEL MUSTO

Italy and the spring and first love all together should suffice to make the gloomiest person happy.
—BERTRAND RUSSELL

No man who has once heartily and wholly laughed can be altogether irreclaimably bad.
—THOMAS CARLYLE

Frankly, I'd like to see the government get out of war altogether and leave the whole field to private industry.
—JOSEPH HELLER

ALL TOGETHER *adv.* All at the same time; all at the same place.

ALTOGETHER *adv.* 1. Entirely. 2. In all.

> The clothes were thrown *all together* in a heap.
> I am not *altogether* satisfied with your explanation.
> *Altogether,* the volunteers for the mission totaled sixty-three.

(T) MEMORY TRICKS

- **LISTEN:** Mentally say the sentence you are about to write. If you pause between *all* and *together*, use two words, *all together*.
- **VISUALIZE & CONNECT:** Visualize yourself as an elementary school teacher counting your children on a class trip. Think, "Are we *all together*? There should be twenty of us *altogether*."

(Q) QUIZ   answers on page 188

1. Are you _____ positive that Henry is missing?
2. We did not stay _____ as a group all the time.
3. I am _____ certain that Henry was with us when we left our hotel.
4. I distinctly remember us being _____ on the dock.
5. I think we were _____ when we boarded the ship.
6. But I am not _____ positive that we were.
7. We were not _____ at the lifeboat drill, and I am sure I did not see Henry there.
8. We went to his stateroom _____, but it was _____ empty.
9. Henry is _____ besotted with Alexandra, but had he deliberately stayed behind to be with her—or had he been abducted?
10. We were _____ mystified as we pondered this enigma.

altogether *See* all together

among, between

Man is an animal which, alone among the animals, refuses to be satisfied by the fulfillment of animal desires.

—ALEXANDER GRAHAM BELL

Among golfers, the putter is usually known as the payoff club, and how right that is!

—BOBBY LOCKE

Whenever I'm caught between two evils, I take the one I've never tried.

—MAE WEST

> There is so little difference between husbands you might as well keep the first.
> —ADELA ROGERS ST. JOHNS

AMONG *prep.* In the midst of; in the company of.

BETWEEN *prep.* 1. In the time or space that separates two individuals or items. 2. Through the combined actions or efforts of both.

Ⓤ USAGE NOTE

The distinction between *among* and *between* lies in number. *Among* applies to a group of three or more; *between* is used when speaking of two individuals or items. Sometimes logic supersedes number, however. Logical exceptions: Sometimes in a group of items, relationships are considered one at a time between one item and each of the others. For example: "I am deciding *between* Tom, Dick, and Harry for the job." In such a case, it would be illogical to use *among*, and *between* is the logical choice.

ILLOGICAL	LOGICAL
My choice is *among* vanilla, pistachio, and chocolate.	My choice is *between* vanilla, pistachio, and chocolate.
There are few houses *among* the three lakes.	There are few houses *between* the three lakes.
She was deciding *among* Princeton, Yale, and Harvard.	She was deciding *between* Princeton, Yale, and Harvard.

Ⓣ MEMORY TRICKS

- **CONNECT:** Connect the *tw* in *between* with "*two* words": *two, twin, twenty, twain, twice.*
- **VISUALIZE & CONNECT:** Visualize yourself surrounded by friends. Think, "I am *among* friends."
- **CONNECT:** *among* → "honor *among* thieves," "rose *among* the thorns," "cat *among* the pigeons."

QUIZ   answers on page 188

1. The pharmacy is _____ the grocery store and the pet store.
2. We divided the reward money _____ the three of us.
3. Warning! _____ the beautiful flowers in our gardens are four that can be deadly.
4. Is that foxglove _____ the two rosebushes?
5. Careful—its flowers are _____ the most poisonous if you eat them.
6. The charming autumn crocus is _____ the few flowers that bloom before they have leaves.
7. But autumn crocus flowers are poisonous and have caused several deaths _____ those who found them in the woods and tried to eat them.
8. The beautiful flowers of oleander and angel's trumpet are _____ the garden's most deadly.
9. _____ the beauties of the garden lie some hazards, but only if you eat the flowers.

as *See* like

as if *See* like

assure, ensure, insure

Some people think football is a matter of life and death. I assure you, it's much more serious than that.
   —BILL SHANKLY

Students rarely disappoint teachers who assure them in advance that they are doomed to failure.
   —SIDNEY HOOK

One should always ensure a pure environment while making food.
   —RIG VEDA

Ensure that your script is watertight. If it's not on the page, it will never magically appear on the screen.
   —RICHARD E. GRANT

> You know, my dear, I insured my voice for fifty thousand dollars.
> —MIRIAM HOPKINS
>
> We can never insure 100 percent of the population against 100 percent of the
> hazards and vicissitudes of life ... .
> —FRANKLIN D. ROOSEVELT

ASSURE *v.* 1. To impart certainty. 2. To reassure or guarantee, often
through words or gestures.

ENSURE *v.* To make safe or certain, often by taking some action.

INSURE *v.* To provide or buy insurance for, usually to obtain financial
security.

> Your check is in the mail, I *assure* you.
>
> Make your reservation to *ensure* you get on that flight.
>
> Does your policy *insure* you against flood damage?

MEMORY TRICKS

- **CONNECT:** *assure* → *reassure*. (You *assure* and *reassure* people, not
  things.)
- **VISUALIZE & CONNECT:** Visualize yourself putting a check made out
  to "*EN*" in an envelope. Think: "*Enclose* the check in an *envelope* to
  ensure payment."
- **CONNECT:** *insure* → life *insurance*.

QUIZ   answers on page 188

1. Do you need to _____ the contents of this package?
2. Send your letter by Priority Mail to _____ that it arrives by Friday.
3. Let me _____ you that I will _____ the vase against loss, and I
   will double-box it to _____ its safe delivery.
4. Be sure to _____ students that our correspondence course will help
   _____ their success in picking the right stocks.
5. Did you _____ your house for its replacement value?

bad, badly

There is nothing so bad or so good that you will not find an Englishman doing it ...

—GEORGE BERNARD SHAW

Growing old is no more than a bad habit which a busy man has no time to form.

—ANDRÉ MAUROIS

It is less dangerous to treat most men badly than to treat them too well.

—FRANÇOIS DE LA ROCHEFOUCAULD

To withhold deserved praise lest it should make its object conceited is as dishonest as to withhold payment of a just debt lest your creditor should spend the money badly.

—GEORGE BERNARD SHAW

BAD *adj.* 1. Inferior; unacceptable. 2. Evil; wicked. 3. Naughty; mischievous. 4. Unpleasant; disagreeable. 5. Unfavorable. 6. Rotten; spoiled. 7. Injurious; harmful. 8. Invalid. 9. Regretful; sorry.

BADLY *adv.* 1. In a bad manner. 2. Greatly.

> Put that coat down, Fang! *Bad* dog!
> Fang, you have earned your *bad* reputation.
> That raccoon coat smells *bad*. (It "stinks.")
> Fang's no bloodhound; he smells *badly*. (His sense of smell is faulty.)
> Fang responds *badly* to criticism.

(U) USAGE NOTES

A linking verb (*is, feels, looks, tastes, smells, seems*) is followed by an adjective or noun: *bad*. **CORRECT:** I feel *bad*. **INCORRECT:** I feel *badly*.

Since *badly* is an adverb, it is used to modify action verbs. **CORRECT:** The team played *badly*. **INCORRECT:** The team played *bad*.

(T) MEMORY TRICKS

- **GRAMMAR:** The ending *–ly* is an adverb ending. *Badly* tells "how" about an action verb and is thus an adverb. Played how? Played *badly.*
- **CONNECT/CONTRAST:** good/*bad* → good cop/*bad* cop.
- **RHYME:** *Sadly,* you play *badly.*

(Q) QUIZ   answers on page 189

1. The musicians performed _____ at rehearsal.
2. She felt _____ about her mistake.
3. He was scarred _____ after a _____ encounter with a grizzly bear.
4. Mandrake was an evil tyrant, _____ from birth, who treated his subjects _____.
5. I was _____ distressed on learning that he had paid me with a _____ check.
6. The audience responded _____ to the singer's outrageously _____ rendition and pelted the stage with _____ tomatoes.

badly *See* bad

between *See* among

brake, break

When you step on the brakes, your life is in your foot's hands.

—GEORGE CARLIN

Living with a conscience is like driving a car with the brakes on.

—BUDD SCHULBERG

What breaks in a moment may take years to mend.

—SWEDISH PROVERB

Take the rope apart, separate it into the smallest threads that compose it, and you can break them one by one.

—VICTOR HUGO

BRAKE *n.* A device to slow down or stop something. *v.* The action of applying such a device.

BREAK *v.* 1. To smash or shatter. 2. To separate into parts by force. 3. To take an intermission. 4. To violate a rule. *n.* 1. The act or result of breaking. 2. An opening or beginning. 3. An interruption from work. 4. A chance occurrence.

> He slammed on the car's *brakes* to avoid hitting the deer.
>
> He was able to *brake* in time to avoid a collision.
>
> Fortunately, the antique vase did not *break* when I dropped it.
>
> *Break* two eggs into the frying pan.
>
> The dance band took a ten-minute *break*.
>
> If you *break* the curfew, you will pay a fine.
>
> Winning the lottery was a lucky *break*

MEMORY TRICKS

- **RHYME:** Don't *quake, Jake*. Hit the *brake!*
- **CONNECT:** *break → breakfast*. When you have *breakfast*, you *break* your overnight fast.

QUIZ   answers on page 189

1. You wish an actor good luck by saying, "_____a leg!"
2. Don't step on the _____ pedal when you're on a patch of ice.
3. The team got the _____ they needed to _____ their losing streak.
4. The car's _____ fluid leaked out because of a _____ in its _____ hose, and the _____ wouldn't work.
5. In a train, pressurized air, not fluid, is used to put on the _____.

break *See* brake

bring, take

> The person who can bring the spirit of laughter into a room is indeed blessed.
> —BENNETT CERF
>
> I bring to my life a certain amount of mess.
> —KITTY O'NEILL COLLINS
>
> Take my wife … Please!
> —HENNY YOUNGMAN
>
> It is better to take what does not belong to you than to let it lie around neglected.
> —MARK TWAIN

BRING *v.* To convey or carry along to a place.

TAKE *v.* To carry or convey away from a place.

> Shall I *bring* my guitar when I visit you?
> Please *take* your dog home now.
> You may *take* our plates and *bring* the check now.

USAGE NOTE

Both *bring* and *take* have additional meanings, but the above meanings are those that are confused. *Bring* indicates conveyance toward the speaker. (*Bring* it here—to me.) *Take* indicates conveyance to a place away from the speaker. (*Take* it there—away from me.)

MEMORY TRICKS

- **VISUALIZE & RHYME:** Visualize a clergyman performing a marriage ceremony and asking the best man, "Did you **bring** the **ring?**"
- **VISUALIZE & RHYME:** Visualize yourself as a dieter at a restaurant, gesturing to the waiter to not tempt you with dessert. "Please **take** the **cake.** I'll just have **steak.**"
- **VISUALIZE:** Think of a plane **taking** *off.* It moves away from you.

QUIZ   answers on page 189

1. Please _____ this letter to the post office and _____ me a book of stamps.
2. In the 1920s, Charles Ponzi promised to _____ investors a 100 percent return in thirty days.
3. Thousands of greedy, gullible investors were only too happy to _____ their money to Ponzi.
4. He would consent to _____ their money, supposedly to invest.
5. In reality, he drew from that money to pay former investors, who expected him to _____ them a "return."
6. It was inevitable that the scheme would one day collapse and _____ the authorities to Ponzi's door.
7. Ponzi's schemes were destined to first _____ him away to court, and from there, _____ him to the hoosegow.
8. Ponzi's stint in the cooler did not _____ Ponzi lasting disgrace, for he later landed a job with Alitalia Airlines.

can, may

And so, my fellow Americans: ask not what your country can do for you—ask what you can do for your country.
   —JOHN F. KENNEDY

You can always count on Americans to do the right thing—after they've tried everything else.
   —WINSTON CHURCHILL

May I kiss you then? On this miserable paper? I might as well open the window and kiss the night air.
   —FRANZ KAFKA

CAN *aux. v.* (formal) Be able.

MAY *aux. v.* Have permission.

The drummer *can* read music.

She *can* prove she's right.

May I use the red Jaguar tonight?

You *may* not step on my white carpet with your muddy boots!

Ⓤ USAGE NOTE

Both *can* and *may* have additional meanings, but in formal usage, the above meanings are those that are confused. In informal writing, *can* and *may* are used interchangeably to indicate permission (e.g., "Mother, can I go to Jesse's party?")

Ⓣ MEMORY TRICKS

- **CONNECT:** *can* with the book *The Little Engine That Could.* As the little engine strains to go up the hill, it chants: "I think I *can*, I think I *can*, I think I *can*." (Not: "I think I *may,* I think I *may,* I think I *may*.")
- **CONNECT:** *can* → *can-do*, "be able to."
- **CONNECT:** *may* with asking permission in the song "Mother, *May* I Go Out to Swim?"
- **RHYME:** *May* I kiss you, **yea** or **nay**?

Ⓠ QUIZ   answers on page 189

1. If you're careful and _____ return it tomorrow, you _____ borrow my new digital Nikon.
2. You _____ come into my garden to look at the flowers, but beware of the beautiful foxglove flowers.
3. Foxglove flowers are poisonous and _____ kill you if you're not careful.
4. You _____ look, touch, and smell foxglove flowers.

5. But don't eat them unless you _____ withstand the stress and discomfort of a wildly racing heart, severe nausea, and cramps.
6. On the other hand, _____ I ask if you've heard of digitalis medicine?
7. Foxglove is the source of digitalis, which _____ strengthen the heart.

capital, capitol

America is a nation with no truly national city, no Paris, no Rome, no London, no city which is at once the social center, the political capital, and the financial hub.

—C. WRIGHT MILLS

The highest use of capital is not to make more money, but to make money do more for the betterment of life.

—HENRY FORD

A prose writer gets tired of writing prose and wants to be a poet. So he begins every line with a capital letter and keeps on writing prose.

—SAMUEL MCCHORD CROTHERS

We have built no national temples but the Capitol; we consult no common oracle but the Constitution.

—RUFUS CHOATE

CAPITAL *n.* 1. A city that is the seat of a state or national government. 2. Money or real estate used to produce more wealth. 3. A letter of the alphabet written larger size or printed in uppercase type.

CAPITOL *n.* The building where a state legislature meets.

CAPITOL *n.* The building in Washington, D.C., where the Congress of the United States assembles.

> The *capital* of the United States, Washington, D.C., was founded in 1790.
> Part of the corporation's *capital* is in the form of real estate.
> The first word of a sentence begins with a *capital* letter.
> Tennessee's *capitol* building sits on a hill overlooking Nashville.

The cast-iron dome of the United States *Capitol* is a famous American landmark.

(T) MEMORY TRICKS

- **SIMPLIFY:** You can't go wrong if you remember that ***capitol*** is a building, because that is its only meaning. All other meanings are spelled
capital, with an ***a.***
- **VISUALIZE:** To remember which word names a building, picture the
famous dome of the United States Capitol in Washington, D.C. Its
shape is similar to the letter ***O,*** and the words *dome* and ***capitol*** have
an ***o*** in them.
- **CONNECT:** *O* → *dome* → *capitol.*
- **GRAMMAR:** *Capitol* is capitalized when it refers to the ***Capitol*** building in Washington, D.C., because it is a proper noun that names a
specific ***capitol*** building.

(Q) QUIZ   answers on page 190

1. What is the _____ of New Jersey?
2. The state _____ is made of granite that was mined in the state.
3. Proposed changes to the _____ gains tax is the topic currently
under discussion on _____ Hill in the nation's _____.
4. Does the name of a state _____ building begin with a _____ letter?
5. Each state _____ has a _____ building where its legislature meets.

capitol *See* capital

censor, censure

One of my concerns is that writers will begin to feel the censor on their backs,
and we won't get their very best.

   —JUDY BLUME

No government ought to be without censors, and where the press is free no one ever will.

—THOMAS JEFFERSON

Censure is the tax a man pays to the public for being eminent.

—JONATHAN SWIFT

You do ill if you praise but worse if you censure what you do not understand.

—LEONARDO DA VINCI

CENSOR *n.* An official examiner who scrutinizes multimedia materials for objectionable content. *v.* To examine multimedia materials for any objectionable content.

CENSURE *n.* An expression of criticism, blame, or disapproval. *v.* To express blame or disapproval.

> The *censor* made sure the script was suitable for family TV.
>
> He decided he must *censor* her speech before reading it aloud.
>
> The senator knew she would face the *censure* of her colleagues for opposing them and voting "Yes."
>
> The judge was quick to *censure* the defendant's outrageous courtroom behavior.

MEMORY TRICKS

- **VISUALIZE & CONNECT:** *censor* → *Oh, my!* Visualize a censor looking at the pages of a book in shocked horror and saying, "Oh, my!"
- **CONNECT:** *censor* → *censorship.*
- **CONNECT:** *censure* → *judge* and the letter *u*. Think, "The *ju̱dge* is *su̱re* to *censu̱re* and rebu̱ke ru̱de remarks."

QUIZ   answers on page 190

1. The _____ deleted a seven-second segment from the TV sitcom.
2. During the war, a _____ checked soldiers' outgoing letters for any information that might benefit the enemy.

3. It is unusual for such a prominent politician to escape criticism and
_____.

4. According to Demosthenes, the most effective way to get rid of _____ is to correct ourselves.

5. What did Juvenal mean when he said that _____ acquits the raven but pursues the dove?

6. Please _____ your remarks when children are present!

7. According to one newscaster, 22 percent of the people in the United States believe that the government should _____ newspapers.

8. Do you agree with William Gilmore Simms that the dread of _____ is the death of genius?

censure *See* censor

chord, cord

When you have thirteen horns, and one is soloing, you have twelve people to play the richest, fullest chord you could ever imagine behind that solo.
> —CARLA BLEY

Every action in our lives touches on some chord that will vibrate in eternity.
> —EDWIN HUBBELL CHAPIN

No cord or cable can draw so forcibly, or bind so fast, as love can do with a single thread.
> —ROBERT BURTON

For people who like peace and quiet: a phoneless cord.
> —UNKNOWN

CHORD *n.* 1. Three or more musical tones sounded simultaneously. 2. An emotional response.

CORD *n.* 1. A string or cable. 2. A ropelike anatomical structure. 3. A unit of cut wood.

> The song ended as it began, with a C-minor *chord*.
> Her kind words struck a sympathetic *chord*.

Tie the package carefully with strong *cord*.

Don't strain your vocal *cords*.

We need to buy a *cord* of firewood.

T **MEMORY TRICKS**

- **CONNECT:** *chord → chorus → choral*. (If its meaning is musical, the word is *chord* with an *h*.)
- **VISUALIZE & RHYME:** A *cord is* wrapped around a *Ford*. Cut the *cord* with a *sword*.

QUIZ answers on page 190

1. Do you have a _____ long enough go around a _____ of wood, which is 4 by 4 by 8 feet?

2. The sonata's opening _____ progression set a plaintive note that struck a responsive _____ in the audience.

3. Fortunately, his spinal _____ was not injured when a _____ of wood fell off the truck on top of him.

4. His unfortunate demonstration of the fire hazards of overloading an electrical outlet struck a _____ of alarm in the audience.

5. The demonstration—which consisted of plugging in a power _____ from a space heater plus an extension _____ to which was attached the electric _____ to a toaster and the _____ to a hair dryer— proved the old adage about where there's smoke, there's fire!

chronic *See* acute

cite, sight, site

The devil can cite Scripture for his purpose.
    —WILLIAM SHAKESPEARE

Those who have heard me speak from time to time know that quite often I cite the observation of that great American author, Mark Twain, who said, history does not repeat itself, but it rhymes.

—J.D. HAYWORTH

After marriage, a woman's sight becomes so keen that she can see right through her husband without looking at him, and a man's so dull that he can look right through his wife without seeing her.

—HELEN ROWLAND

He fell in love with himself at first sight, and it is a passion to which he has always remained faithful.

—ANTHONY POWELL

An architect's most useful tools are an eraser at the drawing board and a wrecking bar at the site.

—FRANK LLOYD WRIGHT

Blogs are a great way to monitor and even participate in the chatter about your new site.

—MIKE DAVIDSON

CITE *v.* 1. To quote as an example, authority, or proof. 2. To summon before a court.

SIGHT *n.* 1. The ability to see. 2. Something that is seen.

SITE *n.* The place where something is, was, or will be located.

> She found it embarrassing for her teacher to *cite* her as a good example.
>
> Will the officer *cite* me for speeding?
>
> His *sight* was impaired by the heavy smoke.
>
> Is any *sight* more welcome than a baby's smile?
>
> I think I dropped my wallet at the construction *site*.
>
> I am having some difficulty designing my own web*site*.

(T) MEMORY TRICKS

- **CONNECT:** *cite* → *citation*.

- **CONNECT:** *sight* → *sightseeing.*
- **CONNECT:** *site* → *situated.*

QUIZ   answers on page 190

1. We're standing on the _____ of the first schoolhouse in Tennessee.
2. What a _____ , to be on the _____ at Cape Canaveral when a space shuttle is launched!
3. To _____ the sentiments of George Bernard Shaw, "Beauty is all very well at first _____ ; but who ever looks at it when it has been in the house three days?"
4. Can you _____ an example of a web _____ that gives information on the senses of hearing and _____ of the various reptiles?
5. Go to NASCAR.com, the official _____ of NASCAR, to see dramatic shots of the Bristol Motor Speedway, an amazing _____ for the eyes, which many _____ as the "Coliseum of Confusion."
6. To _____ the words of racing legend Mario Andretti, "Circumstances may cause interruptions and delays, but never lose _____ of your goal."

coarse, course

For the first time, the weird and the stupid and the coarse are becoming our cultural norms, even our cultural ideal.
   —CARL BERNSTEIN

The bosom can ache beneath diamond brooches; and many a blithe heart dances under coarse wool.
   —EDWIN HUBBELL CHAPIN

You don't change the course of history by turning the faces of portraits to the wall.
   —JAWAHARLAL NEHRU

A golf course is nothing but a poolroom moved outdoors.
   —FRANK BUTLER

> I took a speed-reading course and read *War and Peace* in twenty minutes. It involves Russia.
>
> —WOODY ALLEN

COARSE *adj.* 1. Rough, harsh. 2. Crude, lacking in refinement.

COURSE *n.* 1. A path of progress or action. 2. A route or path. 3. A series of educational materials dealing with a given subject. *v.* To run swiftly or pursue. 4. *Of course.* Certainly; as might be expected.

> The sackcloth tunic felt *coarse* and abrasive on the skin.
>
> Of *course*, his *coarse* language and manners will be frowned upon by "polite society."
>
> The race*course* has harness racing from April through November.
>
> How much is the textbook for the humanities *course?*
>
> Blood *courses* swiftly through the blood vessels on its *course* through the body.

MEMORY TRICKS

- **CONNECT:** *a* in s*a*ndpaper with the *a* in co*a*rse. Think: "S*a*ndpaper feels co*a*rse."
- **CONNECT:** *u* in r*u*n with the *u* in co*u*rse. Think: "Horses r*u*n on a race co*u*rse."

QUIZ   answers on page 191

1. Does the _____ of true love ever run smooth?
2. The film's _____ language was edited in order to show it on television.
3. You'll find Harry on the golf _____ , of _____ .
4. Of _____ , in the _____ of my daily skin care, I always scrub my skin with _____ almond granules to minimize _____ pores.
5. Relying on my _____ in celestial navigation, I set our ship's _____ , knowing that in due _____ we would reach Nova Scotia.

6. We will carry our canoes across this _____ , grainy sand to the river, then _____ swiftly downstream and arrive at our destination in due _____ .

complement, compliment

Guilt always hurries towards its complement, punishment; only there does its satisfaction lie.

—LAWRENCE DURRELL

I have the normal complement of anxieties, neuroses, psychoses, and whatever else—but I'm absolutely nothing special.

—CLIVE BARKER

Whenever a man's friends begin to compliment him about looking young, he may be sure that they think he is growing old.

—VICTOR HUGO

The greatest compliment that was ever paid me was when one asked me what I thought, and attended to my answer.

—HENRY DAVID THOREAU

COMPLEMENT *n.* Something that completes or makes perfect. *v.* To serve as a *complement* to.

COMPLIMENT *n.* An expression of praise, respect, or admiration. *v.* To pay a *compliment* to.

> This wine is a perfect *complement* to the meal.
>
> You need this pair of sandals to *complement* that dress.
>
> Was his *compliment* genuine or was it flattery?
>
> I'd like to *compliment* you on your beautiful singing.

Ⓤ USAGE NOTE

The word *complimentary* is related to *compliment*, not *complement*. For example, "Please accept this *complimentary* glass of wine." ("Please accept this glass of wine as a *compliment* to you," or "with my *compliments*."

T · MEMORY TRICKS

- **CONNECT:** the **e** in *complement* to the **e** in *complete*. Think: "A *complement completes* something."
- **CONNECT:** the **i** in *compliment* to the **i** in *like* and *nice*. Think: "I *like a compliment*. A *compliment* is *nice*."

Q · QUIZ   answers on page 191

1. May I _____ you on your taste in clothes?
2. This scarf is a perfect _____ to your jacket.
3. Early in the game, cereal manufacturers learned to use the cereal box to distinguish a product from its competitors and to _____ its contents.
4. Both celebrities and cartoon characters were paid the _____ of being a product's mascot.
5. Mascots were chosen to _____ the product's perceived features.
6. For example, the choice of Norman Rockwell to paint a red-haired, freckle-faced boy for Kellogg's Corn Flakes, was a _____ to Rockwell's ability to project a homey, family image that would _____ the message, "Buy Kellogg's Corn Flakes for your kids."
7. Even the box's background color, white, was chosen to _____ the pure, clean image targeted for the product, just as yellow was chosen as a _____ for the cheerful, energy-packed image designed for Kellogg's Corn Pops.
8. For many reasons, high sales of a boxed cereal are a _____ to its designer's ability to effectively _____ the product's personality, or image.

compliment *See* complement

compose, comprise

It is not hard to compose, but what is fabulously hard is to leave the superfluous notes under the table.

—JOHANNES BRAHMS

All the choir of heaven and furniture of earth—in a word, all those bodies which compose the frame of the world—have not any subsistence without a mind.

—GEORGE BERKELEY

Courage is what preserves our liberty, safety, life, and our homes and parents, our country and children. Courage comprises all things.

—TITUS MACCIUS PLAUTUS

The Tertiary (surface of the earth's crust) comprises railway tracks, patent pavements, grass, snakes, moldy boots, beer bottles, tomato cans, intoxicated citizens, garbage, anarchists, snap-dogs, and fools.

—AMBROSE BIERCE

COMPOSE *v.* 1. To form; to make up the parts of a whole. 2. To create.

COMPRISE *v.* To consist of; to contain.

> What three branches *compose* the federal government?
>
> Some composers use the piano as they *compose* music.
>
> The property *comprises* three acres of forest and a bog.
>
> The festival *comprises* events for children and for adults.

Ⓤ **USAGE NOTE**

The whole *comprises* the parts. Or, the whole *is composed of* the parts. Never use *comprised of*. (*Comprised* means "included," and you wouldn't say "included of.") Likewise, the parts *compose* the whole; they <u>do not comprise</u> the whole. (*Comprise* means "include," and it would not make sense to say, "The parts *include* the whole.) Some additional "Correct" and "Incorrect" examples follow.

CORRECT	INCORRECT
America *comprises* fifty states.	America *is comprised of* fifty states.
America *is composed of* fifty states.	Fifty states *comprise* America.
The alphabet comprises twenty-six letters.	The alphabet *is comprised of* twenty-six letters.

The alphabet *is composed of* twenty-six letters.	Twenty-six letters *comprise* the alphabet.
The exhibit *comprises* artifacts from the site.	The exhibit *is comprised of* artifacts from the site.
The exhibit *is composed of* artifacts from the site	Artifacts from the site *comprise* the exhibit.

(T) MEMORY TRICKS

- **CONTRAST:** The whole *comprises* the parts; parts *compose* the whole.
- **CONNECT:** *compose → composer → composition.*
- **RHYME:** I *chose* to *compose* an ode to a *rose.*
- **RHYME:** I choose my wardrobe to *comprise,* clothes that flatter and *disguise* my *thighs.*

(Q) QUIZ   answers on page 191

1. Orchestras _____ four groups of instruments: strings, woodwinds, brass, and percussion.
2. She began to _____ a "Dear John" letter to Harry.
3. These two volumes _____ all that remains of the ancient library.
4. Eleven of the finest players _____ the All-Star team.
5. What five large bodies of water _____ the Great Lakes?

comprise *See* compose

continual, continuous

A continual atmosphere of hectic passion is very trying if you haven't got any of your own.
    —DOROTHY L. SAYERS

Without continual growth and progress, such words as improvement, achievement, and success have no meaning.
    —BENJAMIN FRANKLIN

> Continuous effort—not strength or intelligence—is the key to unlocking our potential.
>
> —WINSTON CHURCHILL
>
> View life as a continuous learning experience.
>
> —DENIS WAITLEY

CONTINUAL *adj.* Occurring repeatedly.

CONTINUOUS *adj.* Occurring constantly.

> I am tired of your *continual* complaints.
>
> My New Year's resolution is to strive for *continual* improvement.
>
> The *continuous* noise of the fan kept me awake.
>
> How fast does Earth move in its *continuous* journey around the sun?

USAGE NOTE

The usual mistake is to use *continuous* rather than *continual* to refer to something that recurs frequently but not constantly.

MEMORY TRICKS

- **CONNECT:** the *a* in *continu**a**l* with the *a* in *ag**a**in*. Something that is *continu**a**l* happens *ag**a**in* and *ag**a**in*.
- **CONNECT:** Connect *al* with *continu**al***. "*Al* is annoyed by his colleague's *continu**al*** sarcastic observations."
- **CONNECT:** the *ous* in *continu**ous*** to *One Unending Sequence*. (Something that is *continu**ous*** is unending.)
- **CONNECT:** Connect the *o* in *continu**o**us* with a circle. The letter *o* looks like a circle, and a circle is *continu**o**us*, unending.

QUIZ   answers on page 192

1. The _____ barking of our neighbor's dog is an annoyance.
2. There is a _____ stream of traffic through town during rush hour.

3. She listened to the _____ rush of water over the dam, punctuated by a _____ stop-and-start buzz of a chain saw.

4. Every night, from 8:00 until 12:00, the uninterrupted, _____ loud music from the upstairs apartment was a source of constant irritation, which was not remedied by my _____ complaints to the landlord.

5. The speaker droned on interminably in a _____ monotone in spite of _____ attempts by the moderator to cut him off.

continuous *See* continual

cord *See* chord

council, counsel

Now, I cannot approve anything the council has rejected, but I can reject anything the council has approved.

—JANE ALEXANDER

The council now beginning rises in the Church like the daybreak, a forerunner of most splendid light.

—POPE JOHN XXIII

Who cannot give good counsel? 'Tis cheap, it costs them nothing.

—ROBERT BURTON

It is a light thing for whoever keeps his foot outside trouble to advise and counsel him that suffers.

—AESCHYLUS

COUNCIL *n.* A group of people that meets to discuss and develop policy.

COUNSEL *n.* 1. A discussion; a consultation. 2. Advice. 3. A lawyer or group of lawyers. *v.* To offer advice.

> The safety *council* meets once a month.
>
> The doctors held a *counsel* about alternative treatments.
>
> I will follow my doctor's *counsel* to stop smoking.
>
> The *counsel* for the defense questioned the first witness.
>
> Parents *counsel* their children.

T MEMORY TRICKS

- **CONNECT:** the _il_ in _council_ with "group of people." Think: "_Bill_, _Phil_, _Jill_, and _Will_ are in the town _council_."
- **CONNECT:** the _el_ in _counsel_ with the _el_ in _help_. (_Counsel_ is h**el**p or advice.)

Q QUIZ   answers on page 192

1. When O'Reilly was in high school, he was elected to student _____.
2. Let's hold a _____ to decide how to present our plan to city _____ .
3. I am seeking your _____ on how to find a _____ for the defense.
4. Her _____ was that it was advisable to seek the _____ of an attorney who has expertise in such matters.
5. On advice of _____ , the _____ decided not to allocate any more funds for the questionable project.
6. Her _____ advised her that she should first seek _____ from an expert and then approach the town _____ .

counsel _See_ **council**

course _See_ **coarse**

desert, dessert

All sunshine makes a desert.
—ARABIC PROVERB

People in my books tend to get their just deserts, even if not at the hands of the police.
—ANTONIA FRASER

Being a good psychoanalyst, in short, has the same disadvantage as being a good parent: The children desert one as they grow up.
—MORTON HUNT

Drama is like a plate of meat and potatoes, comedy is rather the dessert, a bit like meringue.

—WOODY ALLEN

DESERT *n,* 1, An arid, barren land. 2. *(usually plural)* Deserved punishment or reward (e.g., "just deserts"). *v.* To abandon.

DESSERT *n.* A sweet treat, usually served at the end of a meal.

> This *desert* receives less than 10 inches of rain annually.
>
> You will receive your just *deserts* for spreading those malicious lies.
>
> I cannot *desert* you in your hour of need.
>
> My favorite *dessert*? It's a toss-up between tiramisu and pecan pie.

(T) MEMORY TRICKS

- **SIMPLIFY:** *Dessert,* with a double *s,* has only one meaning: "The sweet treat you eat at the end of the meal." This simplifies matters, since every other meaning is spelled with one *s, desert*.
- **CONNECT:** To remember which word in the pair has a double *s,* think: "A *dessert* is something you may well want two of, but one dry, sandy *desert* is enough."

(Q) QUIZ   answers on page 192

1. Please don't _____ me on this dry, arid _____ .
2. Harvey received his just _____ tonight for his naughty behavior— no _____ after supper and no television or electronic games.
3. If you violate your orders and _____ your military post, albeit in a sweltering, uninhabitable _____ , the army will see that you get your just _____ which will not be sweet like an after-dinner _____ .
4. Do I have the willpower to _____ this luscious triple-chocolate _____ and leave it alone and untouched on the table?

dessert *See* desert

device, devise

Democracy is a device that insures we shall be governed no better than we deserve.

—GEORGE BERNARD SHAW

Building a mechanical device for its appearance is like putting lace on a bowling ball.

—ANDREW VACHSS

Human subtlety will never devise an invention more beautiful, more simple or more direct than does nature, because in her inventions nothing is lacking, and nothing is superfluous.

—LEONARDO DA VINCI

My first care the following morning was to devise some means of discovering the man in the grey cloak.

—ADELBERT VON CHAMISSO

DEVICE *n.* A plan, gadget, or artistic contrivance devised to help accomplish one's purpose.

DEVISE *v.* To form a plan; to invent, contrive.

> This *device* helps golfers improve their putting accuracy.
>
> We need to *devise* a method to increase revenue without increasing taxes.

MEMORY TRICKS

- **RHYME:** This *device* is *nice*, but will it catch *mice*?
- **RHYME:** Let's be *wise* and *devise* a *disguise.*
- **CONNECT:** the *c* in devi*c*e with the *c* in *c*ontraption.
- **CONNECT:** the *s* in devi*s*e with the *s* in *s*cheme.

QUIZ   answers on page 192

1. He tried to _____ a foolproof plan to pick the winning lottery number.

2. This state-of the-art optical _____ will enable you to read a newspaper from across a football field.

3. Can you _____ a _____ to open a padlock that has a combination lock?

4. During the cold war, the proliferation of spies engendered a need to _____ tools for spies.

5. The need to _____ a _____ to conceal a weapon produced the fake cigarette pack, a _____ that concealed a one-shot .22-caliber pistol.

6. Another such _____ was the fake ballpoint pen that shot out teargas.

7. Since a spy may need to _____ an escape plan, the CIA was able to successfully _____ a unique means of escape.

8. More than a simple _____ , it was an inflatable single-engine airplane that could inflate in less than six minutes and achieve speeds up to 70 mph.

devise *See* device

disinterested, uninterested

Disinterested intellectual curiosity is the lifeblood of real civilization.
—G.M. TREVELYAN

I'm hardly disinterested totally in my appearance.
—FRANK LANGELLA

There is no such thing on earth as an uninteresting subject; the only thing that can exist is an uninterested person.
—GILBERT K. CHESTERTON

You have reached the pinnacle of success as soon as you become uninterested in money, compliments, or publicity.
—THOMAS WOLFE

DISINTERESTED *adj.* Impartial; neutral; having no stake in.

UNINTERESTED *adj.* Not interested; bored; indifferent.

Since you have a horse in the race, you are scarcely a *disinterested* party.

I am an avid baseball fan but am *uninterested* in football.

(T) MEMORY TRICKS

- **CONNECT:** *disinterested* → <u>Doesn't</u> <u>Involve</u> <u>Self-Interest</u>. (If you are not personally affected by something, you can be impartial, *disinterested*.)
- **CONNECT:** *uninterested* → <u>Utterly</u> <u>Not</u> <u>Interested</u>.

(Q) QUIZ   answers on page 193

1. We need impartial, _____ fact finders to help resolve this controversy.
2. I find it difficult to study if I am _____ in the subject matter.
3. Don't ask me about the mayoral race since I am absolutely _____ in politics.
4. Far from being _____ , Milbridge eats up our local politics, although you might expect him to be a _____ spectator, since he hails from the British Isles.
5. Since I am _____ in anything to do with math, I am _____ in taking a course in statistics.
6. To render a fair decision, a judge must be _____ and impartial.

effect *See* affect

e.g., i.e.

One and the same thing can at the same time be good, bad, and indifferent, e.g., music is good to the melancholy, bad to those who mourn, and neither good nor bad to the deaf.

—BARUCH SPINOZA

It has generally been assumed that of two opposing systems of philosophy, e.g., realism and idealism, one only can be true and one must be false; and so philosophers have been hopelessly divided on the question, which is the true one.

—MORRIS RAPHAEL COHEN

The number of guests at dinner should not be less than the number of the Graces nor exceed that of the Muses, i.e., it should begin with three and stop at nine.

—MARCUS TERENTIUS VARRO

The digestive canal represents a tube passing through the entire organism and communicating with the external world, i.e., as it were the external surface of the body, but turned inwards and thus hidden in the organism.

—IVAN PAVLOV

E.G. *abbr.* (Latin: *exempli gratia*) For example.

I.E. *abbr.* (Latin: *id est*) That is.

> This diet includes foods rich in fiber, *e.g.*, bran, oatmeal, and raw vegetables.
>
> That diet limits daily intake of carbohydrates, *i.e.*, starches and sugars.

(T) MEMORY TRICKS

- **MISPRONOUNCE:** Say "**egg** zample" to remember that *e.g.* stands for "for example."
- **CONNECT:** the *i* in *i.e.* to the *i* in "that *is*."

(Q) QUIZ   answers on page 193

1. The fourth president of the United States, _____ , James Madison, served for two terms.
2. Some insects can sting, _____ , ants, bees, wasps, and hornets.
3. Tourist attractions, _____ , beaches, boardwalks, resort casinos, Revolutionary War sites, and the Pine Barrens, abound in the Garden State, _____ , New Jersey.
4. Ascorbic acid, _____ , Vitamin C, helps heal wounds and aids in maintaining health, _____ , by resisting infection from some types of viruses and bacteria.

5. There is a vaccine available for pertussis, _____ , whooping cough, which is a highly contagious disease spread through the air, _____ , by coughing, sneezing, or breathing in someone's face.

elicit, illicit

The test of leadership is not to put greatness into humanity, but to elicit it, for the greatness is already there.

> —JAMES BUCHANAN

You can elicit much more sympathy from friends over a bad marriage than you ever can from a good divorce.

> —P. J. O'ROURKE

Never seek illicit wealth.

> —CONFUCIUS

I think everyone recognizes that illicit financial activities are threats to all of our financial systems.

> —DANIEL GLASER

ELICIT *v.* To draw forth; bring out.

ILLICIT *adj.* Illegal; not permitted.

> Angie's sad story was designed to *elicit* sympathy.
>
> The bill cracks down on *illicit* drug use.

MEMORY TRICKS

- **CONNECT:** *elicit* → *evoke* → *evacuate*.
- **CONNECT:** *illicit* → *illegal* → *illegitimate*

QUIZ answers on page 193

1. _____ copies of the CD are being sold on the Internet.
2. His quote is sure to _____ outrage if we print it.
3. We must _____ public support to stop _____ sales of cigarettes to minors.

4. When his _____ investment scheme is exposed, it is sure to _____ angry responses from irate investors.

5. Once the senator's _____ tax-evasion scheme is exposed, it is doubtful that she will still _____ the support of her constituents.

emigrate, immigrate

If ever again I see this land, I hope it will be with a Fenian band; So God be with old Ireland! Poor Pat must emigrate.

—"POOR PAT MUST EMIGRATE," nineteenth-century Irish ballad

The hunger for land was another motivating factor for the Palatine emigration. ... The realization that they would have to emigrate to accomplish that goal made them willing to listen to British propaganda about the New World.

—KATHRYN PARKER

Contrary to what people might expect, the desire to immigrate is not restricted to the poor.

—ROBERTO SURO

I think we should modify the laws to a point where it doesn't take several years to immigrate.

—JACK JACKSON

EMIGRATE *v.* To leave one's own country or region to settle in another.

IMMIGRATE *v.* To enter a country of which one is not a native to establish residency.

> Giovanni has decided to *emigrate* from Italy to the United States.
>
> He is going to *immigrate* to the United States from Italy.

MEMORY TRICKS

- **CONNECT:** the *e* in *emigrate* with the *e* in *exit*. When you *emigrate*, you "*exit*" your country.
- **CONNECT:** *immigrate* → *import*, "to bring *into* a country."
- **CONNECT:** Both *immigrate* and *in* begin with *i*.

QUIZ   answers on page 193

1. If you _____ from the United States and _____ to Canada, will you lose your United States' citizenship?

2. In 1849, the California Gold Rush prompted poverty-stricken laborers to _____ from China and _____ to the United States.

3. As long as surface gold was plentiful, the welcome mat was put out for Chinese laborers who chose to _____ to California.

4. By the 1870s, gold had become scarce, the economy was in a steep decline, and laborers who been lured to _____ to California became scapegoats.

5. In particular, animosity was directed toward those who had been lured to _____ from China.

6. This resulted in the Chinese Exclusion Act, which barred those who tried to _____ from their homeland and _____ to the United States.

empathy, sympathy

I have absolutely no empathy for camels. I didn't care for being abused in the Middle East by those horrible, horrible, horrible creatures.

—RACHEL WEISZ

I look for a role that hopefully I feel empathy with and that I can understand and love, but also that has that challenge for me to play—a different kind of role, a different type of character, a different time period.

—KATHY BATES

And whoever walks a furlong without sympathy walks to his own funeral drest in his shroud.

—WALT WHITMAN

Autumn wins you best by this, its mute appeal to sympathy for its decay.

—ROBERT BROWNING

EMPATHY *n.* An understanding of the feelings, thoughts, and motives of another.

SYMPATHY *n.* The act of or capacity for sharing another's feelings.

> I feel *empathy* for Sybil's feelings, but I don't feel as she does.
>
> I am torn by compassion and *sympathy* for the suffering of that unfortunate child.

MEMORY TRICKS

- **CONNECT:** *empathy* → *comprehend feelings.*
- **CONNECT:** *sympathy* → *compassion* → *feel the same as another* → *feel sorry.*

QUIZ   answers on page 194

1. They were moved by _____ for the sufferings of the flood victims.
2. It is hard to feel _____ for someone whose misfortune was caused by his own reckless behavior.
3. I feel _____ for those who have a fear of public speaking even though I don't suffer from that phobia.
4. The teacher has _____ for students who have reading comprehension difficulties.
5. He struggled to find words to express his heartfelt _____ .

ensure *See* assure

every day, everyday

It is easier to be a lover than a husband for the simple reason that it is more difficult to be witty every day than to say pretty things from time to time.
    —HONORE DE BALZAC

I have no dress except the one I wear every day. If you are going to be kind enough to give me one, please let it be practical and dark so that I can put it on afterwards to go to the laboratory.
    —MARIE CURIE

Hippocrates is an excellent geometer but a complete fool in everyday affairs.
    —ARISTOTLE

> Music washes away from the soul the dust of everyday life.
> —BERTHOLD AUERBACH

EVERY DAY *adj. + n.* Daily; happening each day.

EVERYDAY *adj.* Usual; ordinary.

> My cat insists that I feed her *every day* at 7:00 A.M.
> Being awakened by a train whistle is an *everyday* occurrence.

MEMORY TRICKS

- **SUBSTITUTE:** Try substituting *every single day* for the word in question. If that phrase works, use the two-word version: **every day.**
- **SUBSTITUTE:** Try substituting *ordinary* for the word in question. If it works, use the one-word version, **everyday.** (*Ordinary* is a synonym for *everyday*.)

QUIZ   answers on page 194

1. George follows the same routine _____ when he wakes up.
2. Since the dance is not formal, you may wear your _____ clothes.
3. If you use this product faithfully _____ , you will be amazed at the results.
4. Undoubtedly you have discovered that _____ remedies don't work.
5. You can apply lemon juice to your freckles _____ , and the only benefit will be to the lemon growers.
6. We receive glowing reports _____ from users of Freckles Be Gone.
7. Since the sun shines _____ , slap on some Freckles Be Gone as an _____ precaution before venturing outside.
8. Make Freckles Be Gone part of your _____ skin care program, and your skin will thank you _____ .

everyday *See* **every day**

every one, everyone

> I have written every one of my novels to convince somebody of something.
> —MANUEL PUIG
>
> I believe every one of us possesses a fundamental right to tell our own story.
> —JOYCE MAYNARD
>
> I've got a woman's ability to stick to a job and get on with it when everyone else walks off and leaves it.
> —MARGARET THATCHER
>
> All right, everyone, line up alphabetically according to your height.
> —CASEY STENGEL

EVERY ONE *adj.+ pron.* Each person or thing in a group.

EVERYONE *pron.* Everybody.

> Alvin ate *every one* of the green jelly beans.
> *Every one* of the five brothers has red hair.
> Has *everyone* signed the attendance sheet?

Ⓤ **USAGE NOTE**

Everyone is only used for persons, not things. *Every one* is used when the sense refers to each member of a specific group. *Everyone* is used in the sense of "everybody without exception." Both take a singular verb and singular pronouns. Correct: *Everyone has* a right to *his* opinion. (To avoid the politically correct but clumsy "*his* or *her*" construction, it is better to revise the sentence and use plural pronouns.)

Ⓣ **MEMORY TRICK**

- **SUBSTITUTE:** If you can substitute *everybody* for the word in question, use the one-word version: ***everyone.*** If not, use the two-word version: ***every one.***

Ⓠ **QUIZ** answers on page 194

1. A fad is something that sweeps _____ away for a brief time before it fades away and _____ of its devotees forgets about it.

2. In 1958, when Wham-O, Inc., introduced its Hula Hoop to America, _____ of the first twenty million was sold in six months for $1.98 each.

3. During the 1960s, with the Hula Hoop® craze in full swing, _____ who had hips and the inclination was hula hooping.

4. Not _____ of those who tried to hula hoop succeeded.

5. The hip-rotating craze was not admired by _____ , as evidenced by Japan's banning it on the grounds of indecency.

6. On March 3, 1939, Harvard freshman Lothrop Withington Jr. swallowed a live goldfish on a bet for ten dollars, initiating a craze that virtually _____ of post-college age condemned.

7. Goldfish swallowing soon swamped college campuses and was indulged in by _____ game enough to try it.

8. Imagine the outrage of _____ who loved goldfish!

9. Fortunately, threats from the authorities slowed down the craze and soon _____ abandoned goldfish swallowing for the next craze.

everyone *See* every one

except *See* accept

farther, further

The farther backward you can look, the farther forward you can see.
   —WINSTON CHURCHILL

If I have seen farther than others, it is because I was standing on the shoulders of giants.
   —ISAAC NEWTON

A mediocre idea that generates enthusiasm will go further than a great idea that inspires no one.
   —MARY KAY ASH

Gratitude is merely the secret hope of further favors.
   —FRANÇOIS DE LA ROCHEFOUCAULD

FARTHER *adv.* To or at a more distant point in time or space.

FURTHER *adv.* 1. More; to a greater extent. 2. In addition to; furthermore.

> Let's drive fifty miles *farther* before we stop to eat.
>
> We need to explore this matter *further* before reaching a decision.
>
> Do you need any *further* information?

Ⓤ USAGE NOTE

In informal usage, *further* may substitute for *farther* to refer to physical distance. The reverse is not true, however, for *farther*. It is incorrect to say, "We'll discuss this *farther*."

Ⓣ MEMORY TRICKS

- **CONNECT:** *farther → far →* near and *far → far* away (to remember that *farther* refers to physical distance).
- **CONNECT:** *further → further*more. (*Further* means "more"; it also means "*further*more.")

Ⓠ QUIZ   answers on page 195

1. Which is _____ from Earth, Mars or Venus?
2. We'll break for lunch before discussing the problem _____ .
3. In the 1920s, astronaut Edwin Hubbell discovered that galaxies around us were moving _____ from the Earth.
4. _____ , by observing patterns of color in the sky and how those colors shifted in the nearer and _____ galaxies, he was led to the conclusion that the universe was expanding uniformly.
5. In 1998, using larger telescopes, astronomers made a _____ discovery.
6. The _____ galaxies were moving _____ away from Earth much faster than expected.
7. Yes, the universe was expanding, but _____ , the expansion of the universe was accelerating, a phenomenon astronomers termed "the accelerating universe."
8. The _____ ahead we look in time, the _____ the distance between galaxies.

9. This means, _____ , that the universe will become much darker and colder in approximately a trillion times a fifty-year life span.

fewer, less

The fewer the words, the better the prayer.
—MARTIN LUTHER

I always say that bad women are fewer than men, but when you get one, they're fascinating because they're so rotten.
—ANN RULE

Resolve not to be poor: whatever you have, spend less.
—SAMUEL JOHNSON

Humility is not thinking less of yourself, it's thinking of yourself less.
—RICK WARREN

FEWER *adj.* A smaller number of persons or things.

LESS *adj.* A more limited amount in magnitude or degree.

> Eating *fewer* calories generally results in weight loss.
>
> If you improved service, you would have *fewer* complaints.
>
> There is *less* water in the lake this year.
>
> In this area, the average house price is *less* than $200,000.

Ⓤ USAGE NOTE

Traditionally, *fewer* is used for things that can be counted and *less* for collective nouns and abstract concepts. Amounts of time, distance, and money use *less* when they are thought of as a single unit (collectively): *less* than three month's time; *less* than 9 feet; *less* than $150,000.

Ⓣ MEMORY TRICKS

- **VISUALIZE & RHYME:** Visualize yourself comparing your two brand-new cars with a garage full of old clunkers. Think, "My cars may be **fewer,** but they are **newer.**"

- **RHYME:** To remind yourself that **less** refers to things that can't be counted, think, "**Less mess** means **less stress.**"

QUIZ   answers on page 195

1. Let's move to the country, where there's _____ noise and _____ people.
2. Because we've had _____ sales this year, our revenue is _____ .
3. Would you like to have _____ hours in a day, as the French once did?
4. In 1793, the French adopted a metric system of time keeping in which a day had ten hours, fourteen _____ than before.
5. Did having _____ hours mean that there was _____ time in a day?
6. Au contraire, since every hour was increased from sixty to one hundred minutes—no more, no _____ .
7. Each month had only three weeks, _____ weeks than before.
8. However, since each week had ten days, each month had exactly thirty days, none _____ .
9. Deliberately designed to cause _____ confusion and _____ missed appointments, this was a most logical system, n'est-ce pas?
10. But the system, a triumph of French logic, was to last _____ than several decades.
11. It was abandoned by no _____ a personage than Napoleon Bonaparte, shortly after he was crowned emperor in 1804.

flaunt, flout

There have been periods of history where it was considered bad form to flaunt your wealth, but we are not in one of those now.

—ROBERT FRANK

They flaunt their conjugal felicity in one's face, as if it were the most fascinating of sins.

—OSCAR WILDE

He is a great master of gibes and flouts and jeers.

—BENJAMIN DISRAELI

I agree about Shaw—he is haunted by the mystery he flouts. He is an atheist who trembles in the haunted corridor.
—WILLIAM BUTLER YEATS

FLAUNT *v.* To show off; to display ostentatiously.

FLOUT *v.* To show contempt; to treat with scorn.

> They *flaunt* their wealth by wearing designer jeans and five hundred dollar sneakers.
>
> We have laws, and you *flout* them to your detriment.

MEMORY TRICKS

- **CONNECT:** *flaunt* → *fla*mboyant, *fla*shy
- **RHYME:** Think, "*Flaunt* me and *taunt* me, but please don't *haunt* me."
- **RHYME:** Think, "*Flout* the *lout* and kick him *out.*"

QUIZ   answers on page 196

1. Don't _____ your engagement ring by waving it in my face.
2. They will be sorry if they _____ my "No Trespassing" sign.
3. If you _____ the tax laws, don't foolishly _____ your mink coat and limousine—especially with an IRS agent living next door.
4. I finally have some wealth to _____ , and I'm simply following that wise old saying, "If you have it, _____ it."
5. Go ahead, _____ me and scorn my advice, but when you recklessly _____ your extravagant lifestyle and _____ conventional wisdom, you are putting yourself at risk for being reported to you-know-who!
6. I don't mean to _____ my superior grasp of the language or _____ your linguistic insensitivity, but correct usage dictates the phrase "to be reported to you-know-whom."

flout *See* **flaunt**

foreword, forward

I was thinking of writing a little foreword saying that history is, after all, based on people's recollections, which change with time.

—FREDERIK POHL

Here I am, a nice Jewish mother, writing the foreword for a book about Christian nice guys.

—LAURA SCHLESSINGER

Don't hold back. Don't be shy. Step forward in every way you can to plan boldly, to speak clearly, to offer the leadership which the world needs.

—CLAUDIA "LADY BIRD" JOHNSON

We do not move forward by curtailing people's liberty because we are afraid of what they may do or say.

—ELEANOR ROOSEVELT

FOREWORD *n.* An introductory statement at the beginning of a book, usually written by someone other than the author.

FORWARD *adj.* 1. At or near the front. 2. Moving toward the front. 3. Ardent, impudent. *v.* To assist or send onward.

> The book's *foreword* was written by a noted Egyptologist.
> The line moved *forward* at a snail's pace.
> That young man is unpleasantly brash and *forward*.
> I will *forward* your remarks to Senator Hodges.

(T) MEMORY TRICKS

- **CONNECT:** the *word* in *foreword* to a book.
- **CONNECT:** *for<u>ward</u>* → *back<u>ward</u>*. Each of these antonyms ends in –*ward*, which indicates a direction.

(Q) QUIZ   answers on page 196

1. The preface of a book is written by the author, but the book's _____ is written by someone else.
2. We cannot move _____ until we agree on a plan.

3. After reading the book's intriguing _____ , I looked _____ to reading what the author had to say.

4. I wanted to find out for myself whether the book's _____ had exaggerated its appeal to _____ -thinking readers, who envision moving _____ to the day when humans colonize Mars.

formally, formerly

I was an accidental actor. I was never formally trained.

—DAVID SOUL

I formally proposed. I'm a good Southern gentleman.

—VINCE GILL

By recollecting the pleasures I have had formerly, I renew them, I enjoy them a second time, while I laugh at the remembrance of troubles now past, and which I no longer feel.

—GIACOMO CASANOVA

I was formerly so stuck into plans. I can now live more spontaneously.

—GABRIELA SABATINI

FORMALLY *adv.* Following accepted forms or conventions.

FORMERLY *adv.* At a former time.

> We haven't been *formally* introduced.
> Although not *formally* trained in music, she achieved fame as a singer.
> Weren't you *formerly* known as Prince?
> Electric appliances perform tasks *formerly* performed by servants.

(T) MEMORY TRICKS

- **CONNECT:** formally → *formal*. Think, "Dress *formally* for the *formal* dinner."
- **RHYME:** Although you're dressed *formally*, please try to act **normally**.
- **CONNECT:** *formerly* → *former*.

• **TONGUE TWISTER:** Although Frank's flabby now, he was *formerly* firmer.

QUIZ   answers on page 196

1. He was _____ known as "Sweeney" before _____ changing his name.
2. Although I have not _____ replied to his invitation, I _____ indicated to him that I definitely would attend his graduation.
3. Winthorpe, _____ casual and careless about his appearance, was transformed after meeting the _____ elegant Caroline.
4. His _____ disreputable trench coat was gone, and in its place, a _____ cut Savile Row topcoat, the apotheosis of elegance and style.

formerly *See* formally

fortuitous, fortunate

Fortuitous circumstances constitute the molds that shape the majority of human lives, and the hasty impress of an accident is too often regarded as the relentless decree of all ordaining fate.

—OLYMPIA BROWN

It's good to keep in mind that prominence is always a mix of hard work, eloquence in your practice, good timing, and fortuitous social relations.

—BARBARA KRUGER

Do not speak of your happiness to one less fortunate than yourself.

—PLUTARCH

Alas for the affairs of men! When they are fortunate, you might compare them to a shadow; and if they are unfortunate, a wet sponge with one dash wipes the picture away.

—AESCHYLUS

FORTUITOUS *adj.* Happening completely by accident or chance.

FORTUNATE *adj.* Bringing or receiving unforeseen good fortune; lucky.

How *fortuitous* to miss my flight, and because of it, to meet you!

You must have been born under a *fortuitous* conjunction of the stars.

Indeed, I feel *fortunate* to be the recipient of this award.

We were *fortunate* to find such good Italian bread.

Ⓤ USAGE NOTE

Something that is *fortuitous* happens entirely by chance. It is accidental, unforeseen, unplanned. Something that is *fortuitous* can also be *fortunate,* but it is imprecise to use *fortuitous* without clearly indicating the operation of chance.

Ⓣ MEMORY TRICKS

- **RHYME:** A stroke of luck, how *fortuitous!* I may become quite *platitudinous.*
- **ALLITERATION:** *Fortunate Fred found* his *future* in a *fortune* cookie.

Ⓠ QUIZ   answers on page 196

1. The _____ circumstance of having a doctor in the house was truly _____ .

2. How _____ to spot that money under the bush just when I needed it!

3. She is indeed _____ to have a loving, supportive family.

4. Taking that advanced biology course turned out to be _____ .

5. This new legislative bill is designed to provide help for the less _____ .

fortunate *See* **fortuitous**

forward *See* **foreword**

further *See* **farther**

good, well

> Few things are harder to put up with in life than a good example.
> —MARK TWAIN

> If you look good and dress well, you don't need a purpose in life.
> —ROBERT PANTE

> Doing a thing well is often a waste of time.
> —ROBERT BYRNE

> The game of life is not so much in holding a good hand as playing a poor hand well.
> —H.T. LESLIE

GOOD *adj.* Having favorable or suitable qualities.

WELL *adv.* 1. Satisfactorily; skillfully. 2. Comfortably; advantageously. 3. Properly; prudently.

> Ted is a *good* musician who plays the trombone extremely *well.*
> If we have *good* weather, it will be a *good* day at the beach.
> Eleanor avoided financial cares by marrying *well.*
> You would do *well* to mind your manners.

USAGE NOTE

Good is an adjective, modifying nouns and pronouns. *Well* is an adverb, modifying verbs. *Well* can be used an adjective when it refers to feeling healthy. Thus, "I feel *well*," refers to feeling healthy, rather than sick.

MEMORY TRICKS

- **ACRONYM:** Here is a *good TIP:* **T**hings, **I**deas, and **P**eople can be *good.*
- **MISPRONOUNCE:** "*Vell* goes vit a verb." (*Well* goes with a verb.)

QUIZ   answers on page 197

1. Do you think you did _____ on your algebra final?
2. Tabitha, you are a _____ cat, and such a _____ mouser!

3. There are _____ methods of fire retardation that work _____ to combat wildfires that typically ravage the Okefenokee Swamp during severe droughts.

4. Although fire retardation methods do their job _____ , however, it is not necessarily a _____ idea to use them.

5. Natural fires are _____ for the Okefenokee and are necessary to keep the swamp healthy and _____ .

6. Fires do the swamp a _____ service by keeping it _____ cleared of shrubs, small trees, and layers of peat several feet deep, whose gradual buildup would otherwise choke it.

7. The burning of peat has another _____ result in that it opens up and reveals lakes.

8. The destruction of small trees is _____ for the growth of the classic tree of the Okefenokee, the large cypress (which is fire resistant).

9. As far as wildfires in the Okefenokee are concerned, perhaps it's fair to say that all's _____ that ends _____ .

hanged, hung

He who wishes to be rich in a day will be hanged in a year.

—LEONARDO DA VINCI

No man has ever yet been hanged for breaking the spirit of a law.

—GROVER CLEVELAND

A room hung with pictures is a room hung with thoughts.

—JOSHUA REYNOLDS

Now like the old Irish minstrel, I have hung up my harp because my songs are all sung.

—JOHN MCCORMACK

HANGED or **HUNG** *v.* Both are past-tense forms of the verb *hang*, meaning "to suspend from above with no support below."

> The king ordered the traitors to be *hanged*.
> The stockings were *hung* by the chimney with care.

Ⓤ **USAGE NOTE**

Hanged is the preferred form when the object of the hanging is a person. People are *hanged;* objects are *hung.*

Ⓣ **MEMORY TRICKS**

- **VISUALIZE:** Picture the hangman's noose that is drawn for the word game "**Hangman**" to remember that *hanged* refers to death by hanging.
- **CONNECT:** *hung* with "The stockings were *hung* by the chimney with care" (to associate *hung* with objects).

Ⓠ **QUIZ**   answers on page 197

1. We washed the muddy clothes and _____ them out to dry.
2. The outlaw was sentenced to be _____ .
3. When hanging pictures, use a level to make sure they are _____ straight.
4. The famous "hanging judge," Arkansas's Isaac Parker, ordered 160 executions, of which 79 were carried out and those sentenced _____ .
5. The keys were _____ on hooks attached to the closet door.

healthful, healthy

Drinking freshly made juices and eating enough whole foods to provide adequate fiber is a sensible approach to a healthful diet.

—JAY KORDICH

Sugar in moderation has a place in a healthful lifestyle.

—CHARLES BAKER

The dignity of the physician requires that he should look healthy.

—HIPPOCRATES

A healthy male adult bore consumes each year one and a half times his own weight in other people's patience.

—JOHN UPDIKE

HEALTHFUL *adj.* Beneficial to health; conducive to good health.

HEALTHY *adj.* 1. Possessing good health. 2. (Informal) Conducive to good health.

> In general, it is more *healthful* to eat vegetables raw rather than fried.
> The puppies were lively and appeared to be *healthy*.

Ⓤ USAGE NOTE

In common usage, *healthy* is used as a synonym for *healthful* when referring to things or activities that benefit health, e.g., "*healthy* air." Strictly speaking, however, *healthful* should be used to mean "beneficial to health."

Ⓣ MEMORY TRICKS

- **CONNECT:** Think, "I want to be **healthy**, wealthy, and wise."
- **CONTRAST:** Living things can be **healthy**. Nonliving things and activities can be **healthful.**

Ⓠ QUIZ   answers on page 197

1. Which is more _____ , cheesecake or fried green tomatoes?
2. If you want to be _____ , exercise regularly.
3. Eat a _____ diet in order to achieve health and stay _____ .
4. Here the _____ climate attracts those who want to feel _____ again.
5. These _____ foods are helpful foods on the road to health.

healthy *See* healthful

historic, historical

Now, 0 for 50 would be a historic achievement on any other team, but on the Cubs it is usually called September.

—BERNIE LINCICOME

If I can generate enough income, I'd like to get a castle, a historic castle that I can restore.

—HENRY THOMAS

Asking the author of historical novels to teach you about history is like expecting the composer of a melody to provide answers about radio transmission.
—LION FEUCHTWANGER

Fable is more historical than fact, because fact tells us about one man and fable tells us about a million men.
—GILBERT K. CHESTERTON

HISTORIC *adj.* Having importance or fame in history; famous.

HISTORICAL *adj.* Of or related to history; having the characteristics of history; based on history.

> The signing of the Declaration of Independence was a *historic* event.
>
> A monument was erected at the *historic* battle site.
>
> This *historical* novel takes place in the antebellum South.
>
> The date of Jefferson's birth is a *historical* fact.

Ⓤ USAGE NOTE

Historic refers to something important to history, e.g., a "*historic* event is a *history-making* event, one important to history. Something related to history is *historical*. A *historical* novel, for example, may dramatize a *historic* event, but the novel itself cannot be *historic* unless its publication had an effect on history: a "history-making novel."

Ⓣ MEMORY TRICKS

- **CONNECT:** *historic* → *historic* moment, *historic* event.
- **CONNECT:** *historical* → *historical* novel, *historical* character. Think: "I would like to write a *hysterical* **historical** novel."

Ⓠ QUIZ   answers on page 197

1. The letter is not a _____ document; its _____ interest lies in the fact that it was written by Martha Washington.

2. The famous phrase "the shot heard 'round the world" is a _____ reference to the opening shot of the Revolutionary War.

3. That _____ shot was fired on April 19, 1775, in Lexington, Massachusetts, when the British encountered American militiamen who refused to disperse.

4. Although there is no _____ evidence as to who fired that _____ shot, it was followed by others, and eight Americans lay dead.

5. That _____ event in Lexington marked the beginning of America's fight for independence.

historical *See* historic

hung *See* hanged

I, me

My partner and I won the race, and I threw my hat into the air and bent to pick it up. Everyone started laughin' because I had split the back end of my pants out, and I wasn't wearing shorts.

—CHRIS LEDOUX

Will I wait a lonely lifetime? If you want me to, I will.

—THE BEATLES

There is only one difference between a madman and me. I am not mad.

—SALVADOR DALI

Tell me and I forget. Teach me and I remember. Involve me and I learn.

—BENJAMIN FRANKLIN

Sometimes I lie awake at night and ask, "Where have I gone wrong?" Then a voice says to me, "This is going to take more than one night."

—CHARLES M. SCHULZ

I *pro.* The subject pronoun used to represent the speaker or writer.

ME *pro.* The object pronoun used to represent the speaker or writer (i.e., the object of a verb or a prepositional phrase).

Sydney and *I* volunteered to help with the food drive.

Herb invited Michelle, Chad, and *me* to the party.

Brett worked with Travis and *me* to sell tickets.

(U) USAGE NOTE

A common error is to use *I* after a preposition instead of *me*.

CORRECT	INCORRECT
between him and *me*	between him and *I*
with Sandra and *me*	with Sandra and *I*

The question frequently arises, "Which is correct, *It is me* or *It is I*? Strictly speaking, the correct choice is *It is I*. The pronoun *I* is the subject of *is* (a form of the verb *to be*). In speech, however, *It is me* is generally considered acceptable. *It is I* may sound "bookish" or "overly correct."

(T) MEMORY TRICKS

- **SIMPLIFY:** Mentally remove any other pronouns or nouns: "(*Jenny and*) *I* volunteered to help," "Herb invited (*Jeff and*)*me*." This makes it easier to decide whether to use *I* or *me*.

- **PLACEMENT:** *I* comes before an action verb; *me* comes after an action verb or preposition: "*I* see you. Do you see *me?*"

(Q) QUIZ   answers on page 198

1. Mark and _____ went back to Boston, where he and _____ first met.
2. Whom do you believe, him or _____ ?
3. Between you and _____ , Andrea and _____ enlisted in the navy.
4. Will you feed the dog for Bernie and _____ if he and _____ decide to go to the fair?
5. Among Dean, Josh, Greg, and _____ , only Dean and _____ ordered dessert.

i.e. *See* e.g.

illicit *See* elicit

imply, infer

But the fact that some geniuses were laughed at does not imply that all who are laughed at are geniuses.

—CARL SAGAN

Contrary to what many writers imply about the process, nobody forces a writer to sell his work to the film industry.

—THOMAS PERRY

From a drop of water a logician could infer the possibility of an Atlantic or a Niagara without having seen or heard of one or the other.

—SIR ARTHUR CONAN DOYLE

We observe closely related species in sympatry and infer how they evolved from a common ancestor.

—PETER R. GRANT

IMPLY *v.* To suggest; to express indirectly.

INFER *v.* To draw a conclusion or inference.

> Did the article *imply* that the senator is becoming senile?
> I did not mean to *imply* that you are always late.
> The broken window led police to *infer* that it was a forced entry.
> Your repeated excuses lead me to *infer* that you don't want to go to the opera.

MEMORY TRICKS

- **CONNECT:** *imply* → speak or write. (When you speak or write, you *imply* meanings. You hint.)
- **CONNECT:** *infer* → listen or read. (As you listen or read, you *infer* meanings. You draw conclusions.)
- **CONNECT:** *imply* → make *implications*.
- **CONNECT:** *infer* → draw *inferences*.

QUIZ   answers on page 198

1. What clues lead you to _____ that Schultz has recently visited India?
2. Does that raised eyebrow _____ that you are a skeptic in regard to astrology?
3. I hope you didn't _____ from my remark that I think you should diet.
4. "Pleasingly plump" was not meant to _____ anything of the kind.
5. Indeed, we may _____ from numerous examples in the animal kingdom that the tendency to store fat may _____ a superior genetic ability to survive famine.
6. You may _____ , however, that I meant to _____ that I find you pleasingly attractive.
7. I hope you will _____ that my awkwardly stated remark was meant as a compliment.

immigrate *See* emigrate

infer *See* imply

insure *See* assure

irritate *See* aggravate

its, it's

This country, with its institutions, belongs to the people who inhabit it.
—ABRAHAM LINCOLN

Government, even in its best state, is but a necessary evil; in its worst state, an intolerable one.
—THOMAS PAINE

It's like déjà-vu, all over again.
—YOGI BERRA

It's not that I'm so smart, it's just that I stay with problems longer.
—ALBERT EINSTEIN

ITS *adj.* Possessive form of the pronoun *it.*

IT'S Contraction of *it is* or *it has.*

> The beagle opened *its* mouth to let out a mournful howl.
>
> Can you tell a book by *its* cover?
>
> Who says *it's* always sunny in Philadelphia?
>
> If *it's* not broken, why fix it?
>
> *It's* been said that you can't teach an old dog new tricks.

Ⓤ USAGE NOTE

A common mistake is to use *it's* to show possession. This is a logical error because a noun adds **apostrophe -s** to show possession. This method does not work with *it,* however, because *it* is a pronoun. Pronouns have special forms to show possession. In the case of *it,* the possessive form is *its.*

Ⓣ MEMORY TRICKS

- **LOGICAL EXTENSION:** You wouldn't write *m'y, hi's,* or *he'r* to show possession. The same holds true for **its.**
- **GRAMMAR:** Contractions reflect speech. The apostrophe stands for the letter or letters that are omitted when words are run together in speech, e.g., when we say **it's** instead of *it is* or *it has.* Thus, never write **it's** unless you mean *it is* or *it has.*
- **WRITE:** Write out a row of *it's,* but in place of each apostrophe, write a tiny letter *i* to stand for the letter replaced by an apostrophe in the contraction for *it is:* **itis, itis, itis, itis.** Read each aloud as *it is.* Then repeat the procedure, reading each aloud as **it's.** In the same way, practice using the letters **ha** in place of the apostrophe for the contraction of *it has:* **it's.**

Ⓠ QUIZ   answers on page 198

1. If _____ Tuesday, this must be Belgium.

2. Can you name this place? _____ name comes from the Middle English word for rabbit.

3. _____ been called "America's Playground" and is known worldwide for _____ hot dogs, _____ Cyclone roller coaster, Mermaid Parade, and Deno's Wonder Wheel.

4. _____ the one and only Coney Island.

5. _____ reputation is well deserved.

it's See its

jealous, zealous

It is matrimonial suicide to be jealous when you have a really good reason.
—CLARE BOOTHE LUCE

Being with an insanely jealous person is like being in the room with a dead mammoth.
—MIKE NICHOLS

A zealous sense of mission is only possible where there is opposition to it.
—D.W. EWING

People are zealous for a cause when they are not quite positive that it is true.
—BERTRAND RUSSELL

JEALOUS *adj.* 1. Fearful of loss of affection or position. 2. Envious. 3. Vigilant in guarding a possession.

ZEALOUS *adj.* Filled with eagerness; fervent.

According to Saint Augustine, "He that is *jealous* is not in love."

Those gossips are just *jealous* of your success.

The dog kept a *jealous* watch over its bone.

The young lawyer is a *zealous* advocate for her client.

MEMORY TRICKS

- **ALLITERATION:** "Are you *jealous* of my *j*ewels, *J*aguar, and *j*et?
- **CONNECT:** *zealous* → *zeal* → *zeal*ot.

QUIZ   answers on page 198

1. A _____ reporter exposed corrupt officials who had taken kickbacks.
2. Wishing to appear _____ , Frank made a show of taking work home every night.
3. Would you be _____ if I told you I had just won the Powerball lottery?
4. Catherine was a fervent and _____ reformer and was known to be a _____ advocate of women's rights.
5. In spite of Alvin's _____ attempts to get to the root of her problem, she continued to feel _____ and insecure in their relationship.
6. Geraldine had become increasingly _____ in her attempts to re-form Fred.

judicial, judicious

No matter how badly senators want to know things, judicial nominees are limited in what they may discuss.
    —ORRIN HATCH

The people in general ought to have regard to the moral character of those whom they invest with authority either in the legislative, executive, or judicial branches.
    —JOHN WITHERSPOON

Advertising—a judicious mixture of flattery and threats.
    —NORTHROP FRYE

A good father believes that he does wisely to encourage enterprise, productive skill, prudent self-denial, and judicious expenditure on the part of his son.
    —WILLIAM GRAHAM SUMNER

JUDICIAL *adj.* Of or pertaining to courts of law or the administration of justice.

JUDICIOUS *adj.* Having or exhibiting sound judgment.

The *judicial* branch is one of the three branches of federal government.

His *judicious* use of humor lightened the severity of his criticism.

MEMORY TRICKS

- **CONNECT:** *judicial → judge → judgment.*
- **RHYME:** Think, "Be *ambitious* and *judicious*, not *malicious* or *seditious.*

QUIZ   answers on page 199

1. Do you believe that all juries are _____ in rendering a verdict or in awarding large sums for damages?

2. Was it _____ for an Austin, Texas, jury to award $780,000 to a woman who broke her ankle tripping over her own toddler in a furniture store?

3. If lawyers would be more _____ in the cases they accept, our _____ system would not be swamped with frivolous lawsuits.

4. Lawyers were _____ in refusing to accept the $380 million lawsuit against Michael Jordan by a man who claimed Jordan looked like him.

5. A _____ provision in our _____ system is the ability to rule on the legality of a law (which has not, however, kept some ridiculous laws off the books).

6. In Alaska, it is unlawful to push a live moose out of a moving airplane. (A moose undoubtedly would argue that this is a _____ law).

7. A _____ use of mouthwash is recommended for garlic lovers in Indiana, where it is illegal to enter a movie theater or public streetcar within four hours of eating garlic.

8. Perhaps a _____ opinion should be rendered on the legality of a Pennsylvania law that requires a man to get written permission from his wife in order to buy alcohol.

9. Likewise, the Vermont law requiring citizens to take at least one bath a week—on Saturday night—should be subjected to _____ review.

10. Some would argue that laws to combat garlic breath or body odor are wise, _____ attempts to protect the sensibilities and health of citizens and to prevent public altercations.

judicious *See* judicial

lay, lie

Admittedly, I traveled with a sleeping bag, but I could always find somewhere to lay my head.

    JEREMY IRONS

I lay in the bed at the hospital and said, "Let's see what I have left." And I could see, I could speak, I could think, I could read.

    —DALE EVANS

I should like to lie at your feet and die in your arms.

    —VOLTAIRE

The secret of staying young is to live honestly, eat slowly, and lie about your age.

    —LUCILLE BALL

LAY *v.* 1. To place or put. 2. Past tense of "to *lie*" ("to recline"). 3. To produce and deposit ("*lay* eggs").

LIE *v.* 1. To recline; to rest. 2. To tell an untruth. *n.* An untruth, a falsehood.

    Please *lay* the dirty dishes on the counter.

    Last night I *lay* down to sleep, perhaps to dream.

    Does that hen *lay* an egg every day?

    Every afternoon, I *lie* down for a nap.

    He appears honest, but appearances can *lie*.

    Did the suspect agree to take a *lie* detector test?

Ⓤ USAGE NOTE

Forms of *lay* and *lie* are often confused or used incorrectly. Examples of correct usage and common mistakes are listed in the following chart.

CORRECT	INCORRECT
I *laid* the book there yesterday.	I *lay* the book there yesterday.
He decided to *lie* down for a nap.	He decided to *lay* down for a nap.
He is *lying* down on the job.	He is *laying* down on the job.
Lie low until the danger is past.	*Lay* low until the danger is past.

 MEMORY TRICKS

- **GRAMMAR:** The verb *lay* always takes a direct object. You *lay* something down. The verb *lie* cannot take an object. You cannot *lie* something down.

- **GRAMMAR:** Memorize the principal parts of *lay* and *lie*: Now I *lay* it down. Yesterday I *laid* it down. I have *laid it down before*. Now I *lie* down. Yesterday I *lay* down. I have *lain* down before.

QUIZ   answers on page 199

1. Did you _____ that wet washcloth on my wooden cabinet?
2. Yes, I cannot tell a _____ .
3. But I did not mean to let it _____ there.
4. The Rottweiler _____ down beside its bone.
5. I'll _____ the towel on the sand so I can _____ on it.
6. Before you _____ down, _____ the remote control on top of the television.

lead, led

Do not go where the path may lead; go instead where there is no path and leave a trail.

   —RALPH WALDO EMERSON

Most men lead lives of quiet desperation and go to the grave with the song still in them.

   —HENRY DAVID THOREAU

If you do not choose to lead, you will forever be led by others.

   —J. MICHAEL STRACZYNSKI

A great nation is not led by a man who simply repeats the talk of the street corners or the opinions of the newspapers.

—WOODROW WILSON

LEAD *v.* To guide the way by going in advance. *n.* 1. A heavy, soft metal (rhymes with *dead.)* 2. A foremost position. 3. Material of possible use in a search.

LED *v.* Past tense and past particle of the verb *to lead.*

> Adele will *lead* the way to the cave.
>
> My joke went over like a *lead* balloon.
>
> An anonymous tip gave the detective with the *lead* she sought.
>
> The tracks *led* from the cave to the river.

USAGE NOTE

The verb *led* (past tense) is often misspelled *l-e-a-d* because it is pronounced like its homonym *lead* (rhymes with *Ted*).

MEMORY TRICKS

- **RHYME:** Think, "***Read*** and you will take the ***lead***."
- **RHYME:** Think, "*Ned led Ed, Ted,* and ***Fred***.
- **CONNECT:** *lead → leader*
- **SPELLING:** Both *lead* and *led* follow spelling rules for vowel sounds. In *lead*, the vowel sound is long-*e* (rhymes with *bead)*. *Led* has the short-*e* sound (rhymes with *bed)*. Rules: When two vowels come together, the first is long, the second is silent: *le̱ad* ("The first vowel does the talking, the second does the walking.") When a vowel comes between two consonants, the vowel is short: *le̱d*.

QUIZ   answers on page 199

1. We need someone who will take the _____ and _____ us back to the cabin.

2. If we had not been _____ astray by moose tracks, we would be there by now.

3. Myles was chosen to _____ the investigation into the mysterious death of Styles.

4. In his capacity as inspector, he had _____ many investigations in the past.

5. Did the _____ pipe lying near the body or the dagger under the sofa _____ him to suspect that Styles' death was no accident?

6. No, neither would have _____ Myles to pronounce that it was death by poisoning.

7. Rather, it was the faint smell of almonds in Styles' overturned glass that was the _____ Myles needed.

8. It _____ him to suspect cyanide as the agent of death.

9. That faint odor, similar to that of peach pits, _____ to the eventual arrest of the murderer.

leave, let

For my part, I consider that it will be found much better by all parties to leave the past to history, especially as I propose to write that history myself.
—WINSTON CHURCHILL

We should measure welfare's success by how many people leave welfare, not by how many are added.
—RONALD REAGAN

I have never let schooling interfere with my education.
—MARK TWAIN

Chance is always powerful. Let your hook always be cast; in the pool where you least expect it, there will be a fish.
—OVID

LEAVE *v.* 1. To go out of or away from; depart. 2. To allow to remain. 3. To entrust; give to another to control.

LET *v.* 1. To give permission to; allow. 2. Used as an auxiliary verb in a command.

> We must *leave* now to escape the hurricane.
>
> We can *leave* our valuables in the safe.
>
> *Leave* it to George.
>
> Never *let* the puppy chew the rug.
>
> *Let go* of the rope now.

Ⓤ USAGE NOTE

Leave is used incorrectly instead of *let* in commands such as *let go* and *let ... be.* The expressions *leave alone* and *let alone* are idiomatic, however, and may be used interchangeably to mean "to refrain from bothering or interfering with."

Ⓣ MEMORY TRICKS

- **RHYME:** I *bet* you'll *let* me *get* a *pet.*
- **CONNECT:** *leave → depart.* Think, "Don't *leave* home without it."
- **CONNECT:** *leave → entrust.* Think, "*Leave* it to *Beaver.*"
- **SPELLING:** Both *leave* and *let* follow spelling rules for vowel sounds. In *leave*, the vowel sound is long-*e* (rhymes with *heave*). *Let* has the short-*e* sound (rhymes with *bet.*) Rules: When two vowels come together, the first is long, the second is silent: *le̲a̲ve.* When a vowel comes between two consonants, the vowel is short: *le̲t.*

Ⓠ QUIZ   answers on page 200

1. Please _____ me help you with that heavy package.
2. If we _____ now, we'll beat the exit crowds.
3. The hotel won't _____ us check in until 2:00 P.M., but we may _____ our baggage with them.
4. I hope I didn't _____ my toothbrush at home.
5. I don't suppose you'd _____ me borrow yours?

6. Why do I always _____ something behind?

7. The next time, I'll _____ you do the packing.

8. I'll _____ it all to you, Mr. Perfect!

9. Now _____ me be so I can sulk for a while.

led *See* lead

lend, loan

Never lend your car to anyone to whom you have given birth.

—ERMA BOMBECK

Never lend books, for no one ever returns them; the only books I have in my library are books that other folks have lent to me.

—ANATOLE FRANCE

It's easy to get a loan unless you need it.

—NORMAN RALPH AUGUSTINE

Never expect a loan to a friend to be paid back if you want to keep that friend.

—BRYANT H. MCGILL

LEND *v.* To give out for temporary use on the condition that it or its equivalent in kind will be returned

LOAN *n.* 1. Money lent at interest. 2. Something lent for temporary use.

I will be glad to *lend* you my car while yours is being fixed.

How much interest are you paying on your car *loan?*

Thanks for the *loan* of your power saw.

(U) USAGE NOTE

The use of *loan* as a verb is increasingly common, especially in speech. Some consider it incorrect, and the British frown on it as an Americanism.

(T) MEMORY TRICKS

- **CONNECT:** *lend* → "*Lend* me your ears"; "Neither a borrower nor a *lender* be."

- **CONNECT:** *loa<u>n</u>* → <u>n</u>oun→ a Savings and *Loan* bank
- **RHYME:** To remember *loan* as a noun, think, "Don't postpone. Pay back that *loan*."

QUIZ   answers on page 200

1. He asked for a _____ of ten dollars, and I was glad to _____ it to him.
2. In the early 1920s, an investor could take out a substantial _____ from a stockbroker to buy stock.
3. Stock prices were rising so rapidly that stockbrokers were only too happy to _____ money secured by the value of the stock shares.
4. It was like a real estate _____ ; investors would pay 10 percent down, and stockbrokers would _____ them the rest—essentially, a 90 percent _____ .
5. Isn't it risky for an investor to take out a 90 percent _____ , and just as risky for a broker to _____ money at only 10 percent down?
6. Because stock prices were skyrocketing, brokers felt secure in deciding to _____ money, confident that each _____ would be repaid—and with interest.
7. They were blissfully unaware that soon they would not have a penny to _____ .
8. Soon they would regret every _____ they had granted; for in October 1929, the bubble burst and Wall Street crashed.

less *See* fewer

let *See* leave

libel, slander

Newspapermen learn to call a murderer "an alleged murderer" and the King of England "the alleged King of England" to avoid libel suits.
—STEPHEN LEACOCK

The courts are supporting freedom of the press, and that's a good thing. We're hoping this sets an important precedent for other criminal libel suits pending against journalists.

—SHAWN CRISPIN

Slander-mongers, and those who listen to slander, if I had my way, would all be strung up, the talkers by the tongue, the listeners by the ears.

—TITUS MACCIUS PLAUTUS

He who knows how to flatter also knows how to slander.

—NAPOLEON BONAPARTE

LIBEL *n.* A written or printed statement or picture that defames or ridicules someone. *v.* To write or print a defamatory statement or picture.

SLANDER *n.* The utterance of statements that injure the reputation or well-being of an individual. *v.* To utter statements that injure the reputation or well-being of and individual.

> The article you wrote about me is outrageous and I will sue for *libel.*
>
> Your paper's false quotations *libel* me, and I demand a printed retraction.
>
> Your *slander* against me will backfire, for no one believes what you say.
>
> The primary goal of his speech was to *slander* his political opponent.

MEMORY TRICKS

- **CONNECT:** *l̲i̲bel → pr̲i̲nt → l̲i̲brary.*
- **CONNECT:** *s̲lander → s̲ay → s̲peak.*

QUIZ   answers on page 200

1. The movie star sued the magazine for _____ .
2. Can a cartoon that uses ridicule to damage the senator's reputation be considered as _____ ?

3. In anger, he uttered some insulting, scandalous remarks that she interpreted as _____ .

4. When you're tempted to commit _____ , close your mouth and count to ten.

5. That contemptible lie he uttered is _____ , and if you print it, get ready for a _____ suit.

lie *See* lay

like, as, as if

I am a woman in process. I'm just trying like everybody else. I try to take every conflict, every experience, and learn from it.

—OPRAH WINFREY

Be like a duck. Calm on the surface, but always paddling like the dickens underneath.

—MICHAEL CAINE

As our enemies have found, we can reason like men, so now let us show them we can fight like men also.

—THOMAS JEFFERSON

Just as the soul sees but is not seen, so God sees but is not seen.

—MARCUS TULLIUS CICERO

Stop acting as if life were a rehearsal.

—WAYNE DYER

Work as if you were to live a hundred years. Pray as if you were to die tomorrow.

—BENJAMIN FRANKLIN

LIKE *prep.* 1. Similar to. 2. In the same manner as.

AS *conj.* 1. To the same extent that. 2. In the same manner.

AS IF *conj.* 1. In the same manner as though.

> She walks *like* an Egyptian.
> She walks *as* an Egyptian walks.
> She walks *as if* she were an Egyptian.

U **USAGE NOTE**

The common mistake is to use *like* instead of *as* or *as if. Like* is a preposition. It is followed by a noun or pronoun (the object of the preposition). It is *not* followed by a verb. *As* and *as if* are conjunctions. They are followed by a noun or pronoun *plus* a verb. Correct: Eat *like* a pig. Eat *as* a pig eats.

T **MEMORY TRICKS**

- **GRAMMAR:** *As* and *as if* take a verb; *like* does not.
- **CONNECT:** <u>as</u> → <u>a</u>ction verb.
- **CONNECT:** *as* → "Do *as* I say, not *as* I do."
- **CONNECT:** *like* → songs: "Mighty *Like* a Rose," and "Seems *Like* Old Times."

Q **QUIZ**   answers on page 201

1. Elsa Maxwell said that nothing spoils a party _____ a genius.
2. You look _____ you've seen a ghost.
3. That looks _____ a diamond, but is it a fake?
4. It sparkles _____ a diamond sparkles.
5. Its price is high, _____ it were a diamond.
6. But does it cut glass _____ a diamond does?
7. Most fakes aren't hard enough because they aren't pure carbon, _____ diamonds.
8. Try turning the potential gem over and looking through it _____ it were a little window.
9. If it's transparent _____ glass, it probably is glass.
10. If you breathe on it and it fogs up for two to four seconds, _____ a mirror does, it is a fake.
11. Thus, if it looks _____ a diamond and acts _____ a diamond, it probably is a diamond.

loan *See* **lend**

loose, lose

All loose things seem to drift down to the sea, and so did I.

—LOUIS L'AMOUR

I'm not concerned about all hell breaking loose, but that a PART of hell will break loose … it'll be much harder to detect.

—GEORGE CARLIN

We didn't lose the game; we just ran out of time.

—VINCE LOMBARDI

Never lose a holy curiosity.

—ALBERT EINSTEIN

LOOSE *adj.* Not fastened or secure; slack.

LOSE *v.* 1. To mislay; be unable to find or keep. 2. To fail to win.

> This belt is too *loose*; it needs tightening.
>
> The elephant escaped from the zoo and is running *loose*.
>
> Did I *lose* my ring on the beach, or was it stolen?
>
> Some games you win, some games you *lose*, and some are rained out.

Ⓤ USAGE NOTE

The common mistake is to spell *lose* with a double *o*: *loose*. This is because *lose* does not follow spelling rules. Logically its vowel sound should be spelled *oo*, as in the vowel sound in *moo*.

Ⓣ MEMORY TRICKS

- **RHYME:** The *moose* slipped the *noose* and is *loose*.
- **CONNECT:** *lose* → *loser* → *lost* to remember the single *o*.

Ⓠ QUIZ   answers on page 201

1. I hope you didn't _____ the key to the safe.
2. The dog got _____ because its collar was too _____ .

3. In the 1890s the invention of the safety bicycle—comfortable, fast, and with air-filled tires—was the Victorian woman's passport to _____ the restricting shackles of house and husband and _____ herself in the joys of two-wheeling it, if only around town.

4. To Victorians, who were so straitlaced that a _____ woman was one who went without corsets, the bicycle was a threat that would tempt women to _____ their frailty, femininity, and male-dependency—perhaps even their virtue.

5. Victorian women took to bicycling like wild birds let _____ from a cage take to flight.

6. Despite heckling, jeers, and even stoning, they did not _____ their zest for the sport.

7. They did _____ pounds of underwear when in 1898, the Rational Dress Society approved seven pounds as the maximum weight of a woman's underclothing.

8. Victorian fashion could not help but _____ o the new "rational" fashion, exemplified by bloomers (gasp!) and split skirts.

lose *See* loose

may, can *See* can

may, might

Your big opportunity may be right where you are now.
—NAPOLEON HILL

Things may come to those who wait, but only the things left by those who hustle.
—ABRAHAM LINCOLN

Progress might have been all right once, but it has gone on too long.
—OGDEN NASH

There was another life that I might have had, but I am having this one.
—KAZUO ISHIGURO

MAY *v.* Auxiliary verb used to indicate possibility.

MIGHT *v.* Past tense of auxiliary verb *may,* used to indicate possibility.

> I *may* go to medical school and become a doctor.
>
> I *might* have become a rock star if I hadn't been drafted by the NFL.

(U) USAGE NOTE

The difference in usage between *may* and *might* is one of degree and of time. *May* indicates a possibility. *Might* indicates a possibility, but one that is not very likely. *Might* is also used to indicate a possibility that existed in the past: "I *might* have become a doctor" (not, "I *may* have become a doctor").

(T) MEMORY TRICKS

- **GRAMMAR:** In general, don't use *may* to express a possibility that no longer exists.
- **RHYME:** Last **night** I **might** have died of **fright**. **Today** I **may** just shout **hooray**!

(Q) QUIZ answers on page 201

1. My homework _____ be in my locker, or a passing raven _____ have flown off with it.
2. He _____ have lived to be a hundred if only he had listened to me.
3. It _____ be that hummingbirds find red especially attractive.
4. If the game hadn't been rained out, we _____ have won.
5. Since Hurricane Elva _____ arrive on Wednesday, it _____ be a good idea to buy bottled water today.

me *See* I

might *See* may

moral, morale

> The darkest places in hell are reserved for those who maintain their neutrality in times of moral crisis.
>
> —DANTE ALIGHIERI
>
> There is no such thing as a moral or an immoral book. Books are well written or badly written.
>
> —OSCAR WILDE
>
> The best morale exists when you never hear the word mentioned. When you hear a lot of talk about it, it's usually lousy.
>
> —DWIGHT D. EISENHOWER
>
> Eating well gives a spectacular joy to life and contributes immensely to good-will and happy companionship. It is of great importance to the morale.
>
> —ELSA SCHIAPARELLI

MORAL *adj.* Pertaining to judgment of the right and wrong of human behavior. *n.* The ethical principle taught by a fable, story, or event.

MORALE *n.* The spirit of an individual or group, especially that exhibited by confidence, cheerfulness, and willingness to do assigned tasks.

> The candidate is an honest, *moral* individual.
>
> Every Aesop fable ends with a *moral*, a lesson.
>
> The team's *morale* was high as the game began.

MEMORY TRICKS

- **PRONUNCIATIONS:** *Moral* is accented on the first syllable and rhymes with **coral**. *Morale* is accented on the second syllable and rhymes with **my pal**.
- **CONNECT:** → "Fine **ale** is a boost to **mor<u>ale</u>**.

QUIZ answers on page 202

1. The _____ of an army is a deciding factor in its success.
2. What is the _____ of the story about the race between the tortoise and the hare?

3. The group's _____ was high because they believed they were engaged in a _____ enterprise.

4. According to George Bernard Shaw, an Englishman thinks he is not _____ unless he is uncomfortable.

5. During halftime, the coach boosted the team's confidence and _____ with a spirited pep talk.

morale *See* moral

noisome, noisy

The body politic produces noisome and unseemly substances, among which are politicians.

—P.J. O'ROURKE

The first flower to bloom in this latitude, when the winter frost loosens its grip upon the sod, is not the fragrant arbutus, nor the delicate hepatica, nor the waxen bloodroot, as poets would have us think, but the gross, uncouth, and noisome skunk cabbage.

—ALVAN F. SANBORN

The trouble with most comedians who try to do satire is that they are essentially brash, noisy, and indelicate people who have to use a sledgehammer to smash a butterfly.

—IMOGENE COCA

Our noisy years seem only moments in the being of the eternal Silence.

—WILLIAM WORDSWORTH

NOISOME *adj.* 1. Offensive to the senses (especially to the sense of smell). 2. Noxious, harmful.

NOISY *adj.* 1. Making noise. 2. Characterized by noise.

> The *noisome* fumes made us gag.
>
> It is almost impossible to talk in this *noisy* cafeteria.

T) MEMORY TRICKS

- **ETYMOLOGY:** *Noisome* comes from the same root as *annoy* and has no connection with noise. Think, "***annoy-some → noisome.***"
- **RHYME:** "<u>*Boys*</u> *are* **noisy.** <u>*Toys*</u> *are* noisy.

Q) QUIZ   answers on page 202

1. At the ballgame, the _____ yells of the fans assaulted my ears, while the _____ aromas of sweat and sauerkraut offended my nose.
2. The room was so _____ I couldn't hear myself think.
3. The _____ aroma of eau de skunk dampened my enthusiasm for picnicking in the park.
4. The _____ fumes arising from a mixture of chlorine and ammonia produce chlorine gas and can be fatal.
5. It is so _____ in that nightclub that you can't hear the band, and the place reeks with the _____ stale smell of tobacco.

noisy *See* noisome

ophthalmologist, optician, optometrist

Ophthalmologists are physicians who perform eye surgery, as well as diagnose and treat eye diseases and injuries.

> —U.S. DEPARTMENT OF LABOR, OCCUPATIONAL HANDBOOK

They don't take eyeballs at the bank. Those who value stocks by eyeballs should go be ophthalmologists, not stock analysts.

> —JAMES CRAMER

Have your optical dive mask made by the opticians who invented them.

> —LEONARD MAGGIORE

And optometrists get to do most of what ophthalmologists do, without the medical degree: diagnose and treat eye diseases, perform minor surgery (in some states), and of course fit people for glasses and contact lenses.

> —MARTY NEMKO

OPHTHALMOLOGIST *n.* A physician who specializes in the structure and diseases of the eye.

OPTICIAN *n.* One who makes and sells lenses, eyeglasses, and optical equipment.

OPTOMETRIST *n.* A health-care professional who examines the eye for visual defects and prescribes lenses or eye exercises.

> The *ophthalmologist* removed the cataract and inserted a plastic lens.
>
> This *optician* specializes in making prescription diving masks for people who wear glasses.
>
> The *optometrist* in the mall gives eye exams, prescribes lenses, and sells eyeglasses.

ⓣ MEMORY TRICKS

- **CONNECT:** *ophthalm**ologist*** → *cardi**ologist***, *dermat**ologist***, *gastroen-ter**ologist***, *onc**ologist***, *proct**ologist*** (all of whom are physicians).
- **CONNECT:** *opti**cian*** → *techn**ician*** → *beaut**ician*** → *electr**ician*** (hands-on occupations).
- **RHYME:** Think, "If you don't need a doctor or ***pharmacist,*** get your eyes checked by an ***optometrist****. (An **optometrist** is not a doctor and can't prescribe medications.)*

ⓠ QUIZ   answers on page 202

1. Take this lens prescription to an _____ , who will be able to make a pair of prescription sunglasses for you.
2. The _____ used laser surgery to repair the patient's torn retina.
3. My _____ called in a prescription for eyedrops that treat cataracts in the hope that I can avoid surgery.
4. An _____ s not a physician but is, nevertheless, the main provider of such eye care as giving eye exams and diagnosing vision problems.

5. I'd take your eyeglasses to an _____ to have that scratched lens replaced.

6. My local _____ gave me an eye exam and offered a large assortment of frames for me to choose from.

7. The _____ routinely schedules operations to correct glaucoma on Wednesdays and Fridays.

8. You had better have your irritated eye checked by an _____ to make sure you don't have an infection from contaminated contact lens solution.

optician *See* ophthalmologist

optometrist *See* ophthalmologist

passed, past

Character is the ability to carry out a good resolution long after the excitement of the moment has passed.

—CAVETT ROBERT

Any thought that is passed on to the subconscious often enough and convincingly enough is finally accepted.

—ROBERT COLLIER

The past should be a springboard, not a hammock.

—IVERN BALL

Those who do not remember the past are condemned to repeat it.

—GEORGE SANTAYANA

PASSED *v.* Past tense and past participle of *to pass.* 1. To move beyond; to move past. 2. To transfer someone or something. 3. To be approved by a legislature.

PAST *n.* The time before the present; time that has passed. *adj.* Over; having occurred before the present time. *prep.* Beyond.

> The speeding car *passed* us at 90 mph.
>
> The quarterback *passed* the ball to the receiver.
>
> The bill *passed* the House but may not pass the Senate.

In the *past*, milk was delivered in bottles.

He went *past* the dairy aisle and stopped at produce.

(U) USAGE NOTE

The common mistake is to use *past* as a verb instead of *passed*. The problem occurs because both can mean "beyond": "He *passed* the finish line: vs. "He went *past* the finish line." Correct: "We *passed* the church on our way to the library." "Midnight passed." Incorrect: We *past* the church on our way to the library." "Midnight past."

(T) MEMORY TRICKS

- **CONNECT:** *passed → action:* "quarterback *passed* the ball."
- **CONNECT:** *passed → action:* (song lyrics) "My Future Just **Passed**," "Love Has **Passed** Me By."
- **CONNECT:** *past → time:* "Remembrance of things *past*."
- **RHYME:** She was *aghast* when he mentioned her *past*.

(Q) QUIZ   answers on page 202

1. Had she driven _____ that same house sometime in the _____ ?
2. A week had _____ since he _____ his driver's test, and he was still ticket free.
3. In the _____ , the senator would have had no trouble having her resolution _____
4. A troubling thought _____ through Vanessa's mind.
5. Had her _____ indiscretions found her out now, after so many years had _____ ?
6. All that _____ foolishness was in the _____ , wasn't it?
7. Surely Kyle wouldn't have _____ her letters on to Lisle?
8. That would be _____ belief!
9. She had trusted him completely in the _____ .
10. Had all his feeling for her _____ ?

11. The possibility that her _____ lover had betrayed her was too much to face.

12. Vanessa felt her knees crumple, and she _____ out.

past *See* passed

pediatrician, podiatrist

After doing *One Fine Day* and playing a pediatrician on *ER*, I'll never have kids.
—GEORGE CLOONEY

Public health educators and pediatricians should make a special effort to help parents who smoke take action, so that their children won't face the same deadly health threat that they face.
—CHRISTINE JACKSON

Like other medical doctors, podiatrists have areas of expertise. Treating an ingrown toenail is one thing; looking for a surgeon to remove that painful bunion is another.
—ERIC METCALF, MPH

The bottom line is, if you notice a change in your feet, see a podiatrist. A podiatrist can test or biopsy your skin or toenails if necessary to make the right diagnosis.
—DR. DAVID BROOKS

PEDIATRICIAN *n.* A physician who specializes in the care of infants and children.

PODIATRIST *n.* A medical specialist who diagnoses and treats diseases and disorders of the feet.

> A *pediatrician* works to control infectious diseases in children and reduce child and infant mortality.
> A *podiatrist* may perform surgery and fit corrective shoe inserts in connection with medical care of the feet.

U USAGE NOTE

The most common mistake is to use *pediatrician* to mean "foot doctor." The difficulty may stem from the fact that many words beginning with *ped* come from the Latin *pedes,* meaning "foot"—*pedestrian, peddle,* and *pedicure,* for example. *Pediatrician* comes from a different root, *pedo,* meaning "child."

T MEMORY TRICKS

- **CONNECT:** *pediatrician* → *pedagogue* ("schoolteacher, teacher of children").
- **BUILDING VOCABULARY:** Connect *podiatrist* → *podium* ("platform to stand on—put your *feet* on") → *monopod* ("a camera support with only one *leg, or foot*") → *monopode* ("creature having only one *foot*") *adelopod* ("an animal whose *feet* are not apparent") → *arthropod* ("a creature such as a snail or slug, that slides along with muscular waves of its underside").

Q QUIZ   answers on page 203

1. If you suffer from corns, bunions, hammertoes, or whatever, call your friendly _____ at FootWise, where walk-ins are always welcome!
2. A _____ can tell you if little Jimmie is just teething or if he's sick.
3. Typically a _____ begins the day with a hospital visit to see new babies and check on hospitalized children.
4. If your son had an earache or poison ivy, you would not take him to a _____ (a "foot doctor"), but to a _____.

podiatrist *See* **pediatrician**

principal, principle

The principal benefit acting has afforded me is the money to pay for my psychoanalysis.

—MARLON BRANDO

A mother is neither cocky, nor proud, because she knows the school principal may call at any minute to report that her child had just driven a motorcycle through the gymnasium.

—MARY KAY BLAKELY

It is easier to fight for one's principles than to live up to them.

—ALFRED ADLER

I've distilled everything to one wonderfully simple principle: win or die!

—GLENN CLOSE, as the Marquise de Merteuil in *Dangerous Liasons*

PRINCIPAL *adj.* 1. First; highest in rank. 2. Main; most important. *n.* 1. The person with controlling authority; the head of an organization. 2. Money on which interest it paid.

PRINCIPLE *n.* A basic belief; fundamental standards.

> What are the *principal* reasons for our increase in sales?
> The *principal* spoke at the teacher's meeting.
> What is your monthly payment, including *principal* and interest?
> The *principle* of equality underlies our justice system.
> The right to free speech is a *principle* of democracy.

MEMORY TRICKS

- **GRAMMAR:** *Principal* can be either an adjective or a noun. *Principle* can only be a noun. It cannot modify a noun.
- **CONNECT:** Think: The *princi**pal*** is my *pal.*
- **CONNECT:** the *a* in *princip**a**l* with the *a* in *main.*
- **CONNECT:** the *-**ciple*** in *prin**ciple*** with the *-**ciple*** in *dis**ciple***. Think, "*Dis**ciples*** spread *prin**ciples*** they believe in."

QUIZ   answers on page 203

1. What is your _____ reason for deciding to resign?
2. The school _____ believed that the _____ of free speech did not give students the right to openly insult teachers.
3. What is the difference between following the _____ of the law and following the "letter of the law"?
4. It may be the _____ of gravity that is the _____ cause of wrinkles and sagging skin attributed to age.
5. The irrational _____ upon which your argument is based is my _____ objection to it.

principle *See* principal

prone, supine

Moon! Moon! I am prone before you.

—AMY LOWELL

One of my fondest memories of the chief is watching him lying prone on the floor at his house, pretending to shoot a rifle.

—TED CRUZ

There is no calamity which a great nation can invite which equals that which follows a supine submission to wrong and injustice.

—GROVER CLEVELAND

[He] was hailed by a supine press as the second coming of Lincoln at Cooper Union.

—CHARLES KRAUTHAMMER

PRONE *adj.* 1. Lying face downward; prostrate. 2. Tending; inclined.

SUPINE *adj.* 1. Lying on the back with face upward. 2. Apathetic; not inclined toward action.

> Lying *prone,* he studied the strange insect crawling toward him.
> Brent is *prone* to be impetuous and take unnecessary chances.

Lying *supine,* he gazed at the stars.

Those who are on guard against their enemies are in less danger of being attacked than the *supine.*

(U) USAGE NOTE

It is the primary meanings of *prone* and *supine* that are frequently confused: "lying face downward" and "lying face upward," respectively. *Supine* is often used in a figurative sense; that is, someone lying *supine* is in a defenseless position and, hence, not inclined toward action, passive.

(T) MEMORY TRICKS

- **CONNECT:** *prone* → *prostrate* → lying on your *paunch.*
- **CONNECT:** *supine* → lying on your *spine.*

(Q) QUIZ answers on page 203

1. She assumed a _____ position to do push-ups.
2. I am _____ to sleep on my back, in a _____ position.
3. He lay down on the weight bench in a _____ position to raise the weights above his head.
4. Harry is _____ to be _____ , to take the path of least effort and resistance.
5. If you lie _____ on the floor, it may be easier to find your contact lens.

qualify, quantify

I was appalled at the amount of study necessary in order to qualify in medicine, and gradually my desire was blunted by a keener—and secret—wish to become an actor.

—CONRAD VEIDT

At the heart of personality is the need to feel a sense of being lovable without having to qualify for that acceptance.

—PAUL TOURNIER

It is now possible to quantify people's levels of happiness pretty accurately by asking them, by observation, and by measuring electrical activity in the brain, in degrees from terrible pain to sublime joy.

—POLLY TOYNBEE

We should not forget, no matter how we quantify it: "Freedom is not free."

—PAUL GILLMOR

QUALIFY *v.* 1. To meet the requirements of. 2. To make more specific or modify.

QUANTIFY *v.* 1. To determine the quantity of. 2. To measure and express as a number.

> What are the requirements to *qualify* for a student loan?
> Let me *qualify* my remark.
> We will identify and *quantify* the qualities leading to financial success.
> Can you *quantify* the results of your study?

MEMORY TRICKS

- **CONNECT:** *qualify* → *qualif*ication → *quali*ties.
- **CONNECT:** *quantify* → *quanti*ty → *quant*um.

QUIZ answers on page 203

1. How can one give a number to, or _____ , the impact and relevance of this research?
2. The number of years it takes for babies' names to rise and then fall in popularity helps us to _____ how long fads last.
3. What must I do in order to _____ as a contestant on your TV game show?
4. We conducted the survey is an attempt to _____ the effects of our new advertising campaign.
5. It is not possible to _____ , or put a measure to, the value of love or of friendship or of loyalty.

6. How can I find out if I _____ for disability benefits from Social Security?

7. In order to _____ for membership in Mensa International you need only score in the top 2 percent of the population on an approved intelligence test.

8. Is an intelligence test, such as the Stanford-Binet, a reliable means to _____ a person's intelligence?

quantify *See* qualify

reign, rein

I find that I sent wolves not shepherds to govern Ireland, for they have left me nothing but ashes and carcasses to reign over.
—ELIZABETH I

At twenty years of age, the will reigns; at thirty, the wit; at forty the judgment.
—BENJAMIN FRANKLIN

The painter must give a completely free rein to any feeling or sensations he may have and reject nothing to which he is naturally drawn.
—LUCIAN FREUD

Ignorant free speech often works against the speaker. That is one of several reasons why it must be given rein instead of suppressed.
—ANNA QUINDLEN

REIGN *n.* 1. The rule of a sovereign, such as a king. 2. The period of time in which a sovereign rules. *v.* To exercise sovereign power.

REIN *n.* 1. A long strap attached to a bit held in an animal's mouth and used to control the animal. 2. A restraint. *v.* To control or restrain.

Shakespeare lived during the *reign* of Queen Elizabeth I.

The king was to *reign* for more than fifty years.

Pull, don't jerk, the *rein*.

You need to *rein* in that horse.

T) MEMORY TRICKS

- **CONNECT:** *reign → king → regal → sove**reign**.*
- **CONNECT:** *rein* → the expression "***rein in**.*"

Q) QUIZ   answers on page 204

1. She pulled back the _____ , trying to get control of the horse, but she could not _____ him in.

2. During the _____ of King George III, Parliament made attempts to _____ in the rebellious American colonists, without success.

3. In 1776, during the _____ of Louis XVI of France, Benjamin Franklin charmed the French court and won a sizable loan for the American army.

4. The hapless King Charles II was to _____ over England in what was arguably its worst year in history, 1666, the year of the great fire of London, in which 80 percent of the city burned down.

5. This _____ of fire raged for five days, and even months afterwards, small fires continued to burn throughout the city.

6. Although frantic attempts to _____ in the fire were futile, the catastrophe did succeed in putting a _____ on the city's vast rat population.

7. So many rats and their resident fleas perished in the blaze, that it effectively put an end to the _____ of the Black Death, or Great Plague, in that beleaguered city.

8. Afterwards, officials were kept busy trying to _____ in citizens trying to lynch French Catholic extremists (whom they blamed for the fire, whose real cause was sparks from the oven of the King's royal baker).

rein *See* reign

set, sit

Set the foot down with distrust on the crust of the world—it is thin.
—EDNA ST. VINCENT MILLAY

> Words mean more than what is set down on paper.
> —MAYA ANGELOU
>
> I don't care where I sit as long as I get fed.
> —CALVIN TRILLIN
>
> Humorists always sit at the children's table.
> —WOODY ALLEN

SET *v.* To put or place (something).

SIT *v.* 1. To rest with the buttocks or hindquarters resting on a supporting surface. 2. To be located or situated.

> *Set* the groceries on the counter.
>
> His observations were *set* down in his notebook.
>
> I'll *sit* on the couch.
>
> The packages *sit* on the floor by the door.

Ⓤ USAGE NOTE

Set is a transitive verb. It takes a direct object. You *set* (put or place) something somewhere. The common error is to use *set* as an intransitive verb meaning *"sit." Correct:* "Sit in the chair next to me." *Incorrect:* "Set in the chair next to me."

Ⓣ MEMORY TRICKS

- **CONNECT:** *sit* → "*Sit,* Rover. Good dog!"
- **CONNECT:** *sit* → "*Sit* up straight!" → "*Sit* in the corner!"
- **CONNECT:** *set* → "*Set* the table." (*Set* dishes on the table.)

Ⓠ QUIZ   answers on page 204

1. Make sure all the troublemakers _____ in the first row, where you can see them, and never let Mark _____ next to Dennis!
2. Be very careful when you _____ down that container of nitroglycerin.
3. Please _____ your books on the counter and _____ down.

4. If you _____ your package on the floor, someone will be able to _____ in that seat.

5. If you _____ the television on the kitchen shelf, we'll be able to _____ and watch it as we eat.

shall, will

I hope I shall always possess firmness and virtue enough to maintain what I consider the most enviable of all titles, the character of an "Honest Man."
    —GEORGE WASHINGTON

Never, never, and never again shall it be that this beautiful land will again experience the oppression of one by another.
    —NELSON MANDELA

Experience is the best teacher, but a fool will learn from no other.
    —BENJAMIN FRANKLIN

No longer shall I paint interiors with men reading and women knitting. I will paint living people who breathe and feel and suffer and love.
    —EDVARD MUNCH

SHALL *v.* 1. In the first person (I or we) expresses futurity. 2. In the second or third person, expresses (a) determination, resolve; (b) inevitability; (c) must.

WILL *v.* 1. Formal usage: in the second or third person, expresses futurity. 2. In the first person, expresses (a) determination, resolve; (b) inevitability; (c) must.

> I *shall* do my grocery shopping tomorrow. (simple future)
>
> They *will* be here in time for supper. (simple future)
>
> I certainly *will* join the circus, no matter what you say! (determination)
>
> You *shall* turn down that music, or else! (must)

Ⓤ USAGE NOTE

The distinction between *shall* and *will* is rapidly disappearing. *Will* has been used to express futurity in the first, second, and third persons by renowned writers. In speaking and informal writing, the use of the contractions of *shall* and *will* makes a choice unnecessary. For occasions when formal usage is indicated, however, it is wise to observe the formal usage "rules." The *shall/will* rules reverse to show determination. To show determination, first person uses *will*; second and third person use *shall*.

 MEMORY TRICKS

- **CONNECT:** *shall* → *the song* "**Shall** We Dance?" (first person, future tense).
- **REPETITION:** Think, "**Will Will** have the *will* to win?" (third person, future tense).
- **GRAMMAR:** The *shall/will* rules for future tense reverse to show determination.

QUIZ answers on page 204

1. We _____ go to the cabin tomorrow if you _____ meet us there.
2. No, I absolutely _____ not do what you ask, and never mention it again!
3. They _____ follow the regulations, or I'll see them in court!
4. He _____ arrive in New York at 6:30.
5. I _____ not go to Los Angeles, and there's no way you can make me.
6. I _____ think about a trip to Las Vegas, however.

sight *See* **cite**

site *See* **set**

sit *See* **set**

site *See* **cite**

slander *See* **libel**

stationary, stationery

Moreover, since the sun remains stationary, whatever appears as a motion of the sun is really due rather to the motion of the earth.

—NICOLAUS COPERNICUS

When people shake their heads because we are living in a restless age, ask them how they would like to live in a stationary one and do without change.

—GEORGE BERNARD SHAW

A logo should look just as good in 15-foot letters on top of company headquarters as it does one sixteenth of an inch tall on company stationery.

—STEVEN GILLIATT

He (Gil Brandt) sent anniversary and birthday cards on Cowboys stationery. He turned most into Cowboys fans.

—MACK BROWN

STATIONARY *adj.* In a fixed position; unmoving.

STATIONERY *n.* Writing paper; office supplies.

> The gym has ten *stationary* bikes for cardio workouts.
>
> A *stationary* storm front has settled over the area.
>
> Business letters are usually written on white *stationery*.
>
> The *stationery* supplies I need are ink-jet paper and cartridges.

MEMORY TRICKS

- **CONNECT:** *stationary* → st**a**nd, st**a**y, st**a**tic.
- **CONNECT:** *stationery* → l**e**tter, p**e**n.

QUIZ   answers on page 205

1. Now that I've named my company, I must design _____ and business cards.

2. As a musician, I constantly traveled, but now I finally have a _____ home next to a _____ store.

3. I understand, though, that the _____ store is about to move, if a _____ store can move, that is.

4. During the earthquake, _____ , coffee cups, and pens flew off the desk, which remained _____ , since it was bolted to the floor.
5. Her beliefs never wavered and were as unmovable and _____ as the giant and noble trees she vowed to protect.
6. "Never, never will I buy _____ made from anything but recycled paper!" she vowed.

stationery *See* stationary

supine *See* prone

sympathy *See* empathy

take *See* bring

than, then

Few things are harder to put up with than the annoyance of a good example.
—MARK TWAIN

It is easier to forgive an enemy than to forgive a friend.
—WILLIAM BLAKE

To thine own self be true, and it must follow, as the night the day, thou canst not then be false to any man.
—WILLIAM SHAKESPEARE

I wake up every morning at nine and grab the morning paper. Then I look at the obituary page. If my name is not on it, I get up.
—BENJAMIN FRANKLIN

THAN *conj.* Introduces the second part of a comparison.

THEN *adv.* 1. At that time in the past. 2. Next in a series or order. 3. At another time in the future.

> Wine is sweeter *than* vinegar.
> My brother is taller *than* I. (taller *than* I am tall)
> I once lived in that house, but that was *then* and now is now.

First preheat the oven, and *then* bake the pizza.

One day I'll be discovered by Hollywood. *Then* life will be perfect!

USAGE NOTE

A common mistake is to use the wrong pronoun after *than*. To avoid this problem mentally supply the missing verb. Correct: She walks faster *than* he (... faster *than* he walks). Incorrect: She walks faster *than* him (... faster *than* him walks).

MEMORY TRICKS

- **CONNECT:** *th<u>a</u>n* → comp<u>a</u>re.
- **CONNECT:** *th<u>e</u>n* → n<u>e</u>xt.

QUIZ   answers on page 205

1. Of all the romances in history, fewer were more tempestuous _____ that of Napoleon Bonaparte and Josephine.

2. Napoleon had never been more smitten _____ when he met the beautiful Paris socialite, a widow, who was _____ thirty-two years old.

3. Josephine evaded his advances, but _____ relented, and they were married in 1796.

4. Napoleon _____ went on military campaigns.

5. Rather _____ brood over his absence, Josephine _____ attended to her own affairs, adulterous though they were.

6. On hearing about it, the enraged Napoleon _____ demanded a divorce.

7. When Josephine pleaded with him, he ended up forgiving, rather _____ divorcing, her.

8. _____ , when he became emperor, Napoleon did divorce Josephine.

9. Hoping for a son, he married a woman much younger _____ Josephine.

10. But Napoleon had loved no woman more _____ Josephine.

11. When she died, the grief-stricken Napoleon took violets from her garden and put them in a locket, which he _____ wore until his death.

that *See* who

their, there, they're

Forgive your enemies, but never forget their names.
—JOHN F. KENNEDY

Even if you're on the right track, you'll get run over if you just sit there.
—WILL ROGERS

Nobody goes there anymore. It's too crowded.
—YOGI BERRA

Parents are not interested in justice; they're interested in peace and quiet.
—BILL COSBY

THEIR *adj.* Possessive form of the pronoun *they*; shows possession.

THERE *adv.* 1. In or at that place. 2. A function word used to begin a sentence or clause.

THEY'RE Contraction of *they are.*

> If the fence is on *their* property line, it is *their* fence.
> *There* are leaves on the golf course, but I see my ball over *there*.
> The Johnsons say *they're* going to move to Florida.

(T) MEMORY TRICKS

- **CONNECT:** *their* → *heir*. Think, "I am **their** *heir.* (An **heir** is going to own something. *Their* shows ownership.)
- **CONNECT:** *there* → *here*. Think, "It is neither **here** nor **there**."
- **WRITE:** Write out a row of the word *they're*, but in place of each apostrophe, write a tiny *a*: *theyare, theyare, theyare, theyare.* Read

each aloud as *"they are."* Then repeat the procedure, reading each aloud as *"**they're**."*

Q QUIZ   answers on page 205

1. _____ are millions of Monopoly fans worldwide.
2. But _____ largely unaware that _____ favorite board game helped Allied POWs escape from Nazi prison camps—thanks to the British Intelligence Secret Service.
3. Operation Monopoly was _____ plan, and _____ responsible for its success.
4. The Brits had a company making silk escape maps carried by _____ airmen.
5. The factory made Monopoly games _____ , as well.
6. Maps and Monopoly; _____ unlikely candidates to be paired in a secret service plot, aren't they?
7. Not to the Brits, since _____ plan was to hide escape maps and tools inside the game boxes and smuggle them into German prison camps along with Red Cross packages sent _____ .
8. They marked _____ "special edition" games with a red dot in the Free Parking space.
9. _____ boxes were altered with carefully cut holes and slots.
10. _____ were extra playing pieces: a file, compass, and a silk escape map specific to the region and showing the safe houses.
11. _____ was real foreign currency to be used as bribes under the Monopoly® money.
12. To appear compliant with the Geneva convention, the Nazis distributed Red Cross packages and the Monopoly games to _____ prisoners.
13. Of the approximately 35,000 Allied prisoners who escaped German prison camps, how many owed _____ escape to Monopoly?   '
14. Since security required all involved to remain silent, _____ number will remain unknown.

then *See* **than**

there *See* **their**

they're *See* **their**

to, too, two

A very quiet and tasteful way to be famous is to have a famous relative.
—P.J. O'ROURKE

I went to the woods because I wished to live deliberately, to front only the essential facts of life, and see if I could not learn what it had to teach, and not, when I came to die, discover that I had not lived.
—HENRY DAVID THOREAU

There are a number of things wrong with Washington. One of them is that everyone is too far from home.
—DWIGHT D. EISENHOWER

Outside of a dog, a book is a man's best friend. Inside of a dog it's too dark to read.
—GROUCHO MARX

To succeed in life you need two things: ignorance and confidence.
—MARK TWAIN

Three can keep a secret, if two of them are dead.
—BENJAMIN FRANKLIN

TO Used before a verb to indicate the infinitive: *to go; to think. prep.* 1. Suggesting movement toward something. 2. Relation to.

TOO *adv.* 1. In addition to; also. 2. To an excessive degree.

TWO *n.* The number written as two; one more than one in number.

> I don't have *to* answer your questions.
> Does this bus go *to* Albuquerque?
> Not only is that hat *too* expensive, but the shoes are *too!*
> Is there a discount if I buy *two* kittens?

T MEMORY TRICKS

- **GRAMMAR:** *To* is followed by another word; it should not end a sentence. In an infinitive (verb form), it is followed by a verb: *to go.* As a preposition, it is followed by a noun or pronoun: *to Joe; to them.*
- **CONNECT:** *too → too many.* *To* and *too* are frequently confused. To remember that *too* means "excessive," think, "*Too* has *too* many *o*'s. It has one extra *o.*"
- **CONNECT:** *two → twin, twelve, twenty, twice.*

Q QUIZ   answers on page 206

1. Elvis Presley was no stranger _____ guns.
2. In 1970, he went _____ the White House unannounced _____ petition President Richard Nixon _____ appoint him as an undercover agent _____ investigate not only drug abuse but Communist brainwashing techniques, _____ .
3. Elvis went prepared, packing _____ handguns, one for himself, the other _____ give _____ Nixon, who might need protection, _____ .
4. Not _____ be outdone, Nixon gave a gift _____ Presley—a Special Assistant badge from the Bureau of Narcotics and Dangerous Drugs.
5. The FBI got into the act, _____ , and gave Presley permits _____ carry firearms in every state _____ assist him in pursuing his undercover work.
6. Elvis kept his firearms readily available at home in Graceland, _____ .
7. He was known _____ shoot his TV set whenever Mel Tormé came on the screen.
8. This treatment was accorded _____ Robert Goulet _____ .
9. His car, _____ , fell victim _____ Elvis's gun-toting temper.
10. When it refused _____ start, he shot it.

too *See* to

two *See* to

vain, vein

The finest words in the world are only vain sounds if you cannot comprehend them.

—ANATOLE FRANCE

He does not live in vain who employs his wealth, his thought, and his speech to advance the good of others.

—HINDU PROVERB

I have seen the movement of the sinews of the sky, and the blood coursing in the veins of the moon.

—ALLAMA IQBAL

Integrity is the lifeblood of democracy. Deceit is a poison in its veins.

—EDWARD KENNEDY

VAIN *adj.* 1. Unsuccessful, futile. 2. Without worth or substance. 3. Exhibiting excessive pride in one's appearance or accomplishments.

VEIN *n.* 1. A blood vessel in which blood travels to the heart. 2. A long strip or crack. 3. A turn of attitude or mood.

> The rescue attempt was in *vain*.
>
> She is so *vain* that she takes every remark as a compliment.
>
> If you cut a *vein*, it does not spurt blood as an artery does.

Ⓣ MEMORY TRICKS

- **CONNECT:** *vain* → *vanity*.
- **RHYME:** Think, "There is no *gain* to be so *vain*, to look on others with *disdain*."
- **CONNECT:** *vein* → blood *vessel*.

Ⓠ QUIZ   answers on page 206

1. Those are _____ promises, entirely without substance.
2. The prospectors struck a _____ of silver.

3. In a more serious _____ , here are the latest figures on inflation.

4. Alvin's three previous attempts to pass his driver's test were in _____.

5. The nurse drew blood from a _____ in his left arm.

6. Although quite beautiful, she was not _____ about her appearance.

vein *See* vain

was, were

If we knew what it was we were doing, it would not be called research, would it?
—ALBERT EINSTEIN

I remember the time I was kidnapped and they sent a piece of my finger to my father. He said he wanted more proof.
—RODNEY DANGERFIELD

If I were two-faced, would I be wearing this one?
—ABRAHAM LINCOLN

If all economists were laid end to end, they would not reach a conclusion.
—GEORGE BERNARD SHAW

WAS *v.* Past tense of the verb *to be,* first and third person singular.

WERE *v.* 1. Past tense of the verb *to be,* all plurals and second person singular. 2. Subjunctive of the verb *to be* (indicates a condition "contrary to fact").

I'm sorry I *was* late, but he *was* late, too.

What *were* we thinking when we invited him!

If only I *were* sixteen again. I wish I *were.*

Ⓤ USAGE NOTE

Two common mistakes occur in using *was/were.* The first is to use *was* with the second person (*you*) or with plural pronouns.

CORRECT	INCORRECT
You *were* right and I *was* wrong.	You *was* right, and I *was* wrong.

They *were* angry, but he *was* not.	They *was* angry, but he *was* not.

The other mistake is to use *was* instead of *were* to express a condition that is hypothetical or contrary to fact. Clue words for the use of *were* include: *if, I wish, would, as, as if,* and *though.* The traditional rule is to use *were* to indicate that the condition is false, contrary to fact. It is also traditional to use *was* after *whether.*

CORRECT	INCORRECT
If I *were* you, I'd save my money. (Condition contrary to fact; the fact is, I'm not you.)	If I *was* you, I'd save my money.
I wondered *whether* she *was* lying. I wondered *whether* she *were* lying. (Correct, but **whether ... was** is a traditional usage.)	

(T) MEMORY TRICKS

- **SONGS:** To remember that "*you **were**"* is correct (not "*you was*") think of the song titles "You ***Were*** Always on My Mind" and "Wish You ***Were*** Here."
- **SONGS:** To remember that ***were*** (not *was*) indicates a condition contrary to fact, think of the song title "If I ***Were*** a Rich Man."

(Q) QUIZ   answers on page 206

1. When you _____ in Hoboken, I _____ in Hackensack.
2. It _____ fate.
3. You and I _____ in the right place, and it _____ the right time.
4. You _____ gorgeous and I _____ rich.
5. Together we _____ perfect.
6. What _____ it the poet wrote ... something about if paradise _____ now?

7. Oh, if only I _____ a poet and my words _____ poems!

8. Whether we _____ fools or dreamers—it matters not.

9. We _____ in love.

10. Or, if it _____ not love, it _____ something quite like it.

11. _____ it to last?

12. Alas, life is not perfect; if only it _____ !

weather, whether

Climate is what we expect, weather is what we get.

> —MARK TWAIN

Conversation about the weather is the last refuge of the unimaginative.

> —OSCAR WILDE

We will act consistently with our view of who we truly are, whether that view is accurate or not.

> —TONY ROBBINS

It's not whether you get knocked down, it's whether you get up.

> —VINCE LOMBARDI

WEATHER *n.* 1. The state of atmospheric conditions. 2. Disagreeable atmospheric conditions. *v.* To endure unfavorable conditions.

WHETHER *conj.* 1. If it is the case that. 2. Used to introduce an option or alternative.

> The *weather* forecast said "scattered showers."
>
> She was determined to *weather* the latest family crisis.
>
> Please find out *whether* the museum is open.
>
> It is immaterial to me *whether* we go to Reno or Rio.

MEMORY TRICKS

- **PRONUNCIATION:** The common mistake is to spell *whether* like *weather* because *whether* is often mispronounced so that the two words sound the same. The *wh* in *whether* is pronounced like the *wh* in *where* (Both

129

words begin with the same sound (*hw*). Practice repeating <u>*wh*</u>*ere,* <u>*wheth-*</u>*er* until the correct pronunciation of **whether** sounds right to you.

- **ALLITERATION:** Practice saying the following sentence aloud, paying special attention to the *wh*'s: <u>*Wh*</u>*ether* or not <u>*Wh*</u>*itney* drinks <u>*wh*</u>*isky* or <u>*wh*</u>*atever* is of no importance to me.

QUIZ   answers on page 207

1. I don't know _____ to wash the car today or wait until the _____ cooperates.
2. Grit your teeth and _____ the storm, _____ or not you're frightened.
3. No matter _____ it rains, sleets, or snows, you know you'll have _____ .
4. They say Los Angeles never has _____ , but I don't know _____ or not I agree with that.
5. It doesn't matter _____ the _____ is good or bad, everybody talks about it.

well *See* good

were *See* was

whether *See* weather

which *See* who

who, which, that

A friend is one who knows you and loves you just the same.
—ELBERT HUBBARD

The person who can bring the spirit of laughter into a room is indeed blessed.
—BENNETT CERF

The essence of childhood, of course, is play, which my friends and I did endlessly on streets that we reluctantly shared with traffic.
—BILL COSBY

> Nonviolence, which is the quality of the heart, cannot come by an appeal to the brain.
>
> —MAHATMA GANDHI
>
> Any society that would give up a little liberty to gain a little security will deserve neither and lose both.
>
> —BENJAMIN FRANKLIN

WHO 1. Interrogative pronoun: *Who?* 2. Relative pronoun: the person or persons that.

WHICH Relative pronoun in a nonrestrictive clause (one that gives additional information that is nonessential and could be left out).

THAT Relative pronoun in a restrictive clause (one that is essential to sentence meaning).

> Hilda, *who* is my cousin, goes to the University of Iowa.
>
> I turned on WBIR, *which* is my favorite channel.
>
> Is this the face *that* launched a thousand ships?

(U) USAGE NOTE

Who (or *whom*) refers to people. *Which* refers to animals or things and begins a clause that gives nonessential information.

(T) MEMORY TRICKS

- **CONNECT:** To remember that *who* refers to a person, think, "*Who's who?*"
- **GRAMMAR:** To choose between *which* and *that*, drop the clause the word introduces from the sentence. If the sentence sense is unchanged, choose *which*. If the clause was necessary for meaning, choose *that*.

(Q) QUIZ   answers on page 207

1. Judo is not an activity _____ one usually associates with presidents.

2. Yet our twenty-sixth president, ———— was Theodore Roosevelt, was a judo enthusiast.

3. Few know ———— Theodore Roosevelt was America's first judo Brown Belt.

4. Roosevelt practiced in the White House basement, ———— he covered with training mats.

5. He practiced with anyone ———— was available, including his wife and sister-in-law.

6. Once during a boring official lunch, he threw the visiting Swiss minister to the floor and demonstrated a judo hold, a diversion ———— delighted his guests.

7. Passing the first workers' compensation bill and pushing for stricter child-labor laws ensured the president's popularity, ———— was bolstered further when he went hunting in Mississippi and refused to shoot a black bear cub.

8. This story, ———— touched America's heart, had an interesting result.

9. People began naming their stuffed toy bears "Teddy," ———— is a name ———— has stuck.

who, whom

A man who has no imagination has no wings.

—MUHAMMAD ALI

Nothing is impossible for the man who doesn't have to do it himself.

—A.H. WEILER

Have I reached the party to whom I am speaking?

—LILY TOMLIN AS "ERNESTINE"

Tell me whom you love, and I'll tell you who you are.

—CREOLE PROVERB

WHO 1. Interrogative pronoun: *Who?* 2. Relative pronoun: the person or persons that.

WHOM *pro.* The objective case of *who* (object of a verb or preposition).

Who stole the plans?

Sebastian is the spy *who* stole the plans.

He is the spy *whom* our agent contacted.

He is the one to *whom* we gave false information.

Ⓤ USAGE NOTE

Who is always the subject of a verb. *Whom* is always the object of a verb or a preposition. The mistake considered most objectionable is using *who* after a preposition (e.g., "the man to *who*").

Ⓣ MEMORY TRICKS

- **SUBSTITUTION:** To check on the usage of ***who,*** see if it could refer to the subject pronoun *he, she,* or *they.* Example: "spy ***who*** stole our plans"; "*he* stole our plans." *Substitution:* To check on the usage of ***whom,*** see if it could refer to the object pronoun *him, her,* or *them.* Example: "***whom*** our agent contacted"; "our agent contacted *him.*"
- **CONNECT:** Think of the book title <u>For **Whom**</u> *the Bell Tolls* to remember that *whom* follows a preposition.

Ⓠ QUIZ   answers on page 207

1. Did you see _____ left the package at the door?
2. To _____ is the package addressed—and _____ is the sender?
3. Ralph, _____ first noticed the suspicious package, is not one _____ is easily rattled.
4. He is, however, someone _____ easily leaps to false conclusions, and to _____ a number of false alarms in the form of 911 calls have been attributed.
5. Perhaps this is only to be expected from one _____ devours spy novels and tales of espionage.
6. He is a person for _____ I have the utmost respect and _____ I hold in deepest regard.

7. Yet Ralph is someone _____ prefers to live life as fiction, someone _____ likes to believe that behind every occurrence lurks a spy.

whom *See* who

who's, whose

You're not the only one who's made mistakes, but they're the only things that you can truly call your own.

—BILLY JOEL

I like a man who's good, but not too good—for the good die young, and I hate a dead one.

—MAE WEST

Never go to a doctor whose office plants have died.

—ERMA BOMBECK

I have friends in overalls whose friendship I would not swap for the favor of the kings of the world.

—THOMAS A. EDISON

WHO'S Contraction of *who is* or *who has.*

WHOSE The possessive form of *who.*

> Who's on first base? *(who is)*
> Who's been sitting in my chair? *(who has)*
> Whose book is this?
> Whose side are you on?

(T) MEMORY TRICKS

- **WRITE:** Write out a row of the word *who's,* but in place of each apostrophe, write a tiny *i: whois, whois, whois, whois.* Read each aloud as "*who is*" and then as "*who's.*" Repeat the procedure, substituting a tiny *ha* for the apostrophe and reading each aloud as "*who has*" and then as "*who's.*"
- **VISUALIZE:** The word *whose* contains the word *hose.* To remember that *whose* shows possession, visualize yourself holding up a rubber hose and asking, "*Whose hose is this?*"

- **REPLACE:** If you are unsure whether **who's** or **whose** is correct, replace the word with **who is**. If the sentence makes sense, write **who's**. If not, write **whose**.

QUIZ   answers on page 207

1. _____ the teacher _____ been most influential in your life?
2. It was Ms. Gillespie, _____ words inspired me and _____ always been a role model for me.
3. He's one of those people _____ face is familiar but _____ name escapes me.
4. _____ the author of that book about Captain Ahab, _____ nemesis was a giant white whale?
5. _____ got a suggestion on a good book to read at the beach?
6. I want one _____ plot is thrilling, a real page-turner.
7. Have you read _____ *Watching the Store*?
8. It's a spine-tingling psychological thriller by an author _____ not only a psychologist but a forensic pathologist, and _____ numerous honors include seven national and ten regional awards.

whose *See* **who's**

will *See* **shall**

your, you're

The best way to make your dreams come true is to wake up!
   —PAUL VALERY
If you're not making mistakes, then you're not doing anything.
   —JOHN WOODEN
You're only as good as your last haircut.
   —FRAN LEBOWITZ
You know you're old if your walker has an air bag.
   —PHYLLIS DILLER

YOUR *adj.* The possessive form of the pronoun *you.*

YOU'RE Contraction of *you are.*

> This is your lucky day; your ticket has the winning number.
> You're not going to believe this, but you're the winner!

Ⓤ USAGE NOTE

The words *your* and *you're* are frequently confused because they sound alike, they have similar spellings, and both appear to be possessives. Although an apostrophe signals possession in nouns, pronouns have their own possessive forms. *Your* is the possessive form of *you.* In the case of pronouns, an apostrophe signals a contraction.

Ⓣ MEMORY TRICKS

- **EXPERIMENT:** When deciding whether to write *your* or *you're,* first try substituting *you are.* If that makes sense in the sentence, use the contraction, *you're.* If not, use *your.*
- **CONNECT:** *your* → *our.* The word *your* has the smaller word *our* in it. Both are pronouns that show possession (*your* family, *our* family).
- **WRITE:** Write out a row of the word *you're,* but in place of each apostrophe, write a tiny *a*: *youare, youare, youare.* Read each aloud as *"you are"* and then as *"you're."*

Ⓠ QUIZ   answers on page 208

1. Let a smile be _____ umbrella on a rainy day.
2. Keep on smiling, for when _____ smiling, the whole world smiles with you.
3. What is that song _____ singing?
4. Is it, " _____ No One If _____ Not on Twitter"?
5. Or is it, "If _____ happy and you know it, clap _____ hands"?
6. I guess _____ tone deaf.

7. Actually, I was singing, " _____ Going to Get _____ Fingers Burned."

8. It's my second favorite song after " _____ So Vain."

9. If _____ tastes run to country and western, try, "When you leave, walk out backwards so I'll think _____ walking in."

10. Or, what about, "You Can't Have _____ Kate and Edith Too"?

11. Then there's, "My John Deere Was Breaking _____ Field, While _____ Dear John Was Breaking My Heart."

12. Finally, here's an oldie but goodie, "You Changed _____ Name from Brown to Jones, and Mine from Brown to Blue."

you're *See* **your**

04

CONQUER 52 COMMONLY MISUSED WORDS

Are you guilty of word misuse? Most of us are from time to time. We misuse a word when we think we know what it means but we really don't. Unknowingly, we use it with a mistaken meaning—and may continue to do so for years. Where do these mistaken meanings come from? Often, they come from others. When a word is commonly misused, its misuse begins to sound and look right. Thus, its misusage is passed on. Usage errors are easy to perpetuate—somewhat like a virus.

Fortunately, such usage errors are easy to correct. Usually all it takes is to become aware of them. In light of that, the chart below explains the real meanings of fifty-two commonly misused words. Acquaint yourself with them and you will be ahead of the game—one of the few who knows how to use them correctly and is aware of what they really mean.

ACCESS	Mistakenly used to mean "an amount beyond what is needed, an *excess.*"
	INCORRECT: There is an additional charge for access baggage.
	Access means "the right to enter or make use of; a means of entering, passage."
	CORRECT: You do not have the legal right to access those documents.

ADVERSE	Mistakenly used to mean "opposed to; reluctant, *averse*."
	INCORRECT: I am not adverse to occasional exercise.
	Adverse means "hostile to; unfavorable."
	CORRECT: The playwright was stung by the critic's adverse comments. The game was postponed due to adverse weather conditions.
ALIBI	Mistakenly used to mean "an excuse."
	INCORRECT: What is your alibi for being late last night?
	Alibi means "a defense plea of having been elsewhere when an act was committed."
	CORRECT: What alibi did Higgins give for where he was the night of the crime?
ALTERCATION	Mistakenly used to mean "a physical fight."
	INCORRECT: Three people were injured in the altercation that broke out between demonstrators and onlookers.
	Altercation means "a noisy quarrel, a dispute."
	CORRECT: Our conversation was interrupted by a noisy altercation between the waiter and a patron.
AMBIVALENT	Mistakenly used to mean "I don't care one way or another."
	INCORRECT: *I'm ambivalent about which movie to see. Either one is fine.*
	Ambivalent means "having mutually conflicting thoughts or feelings."
	CORRECT: His ambivalent feelings about marriage prevented him from popping the question.
ANALOGOUS	Mistakenly used as a synonym for *similar*. *Analogous* means "similarity in some respects from things that are otherwise dissimilar."
	CORRECT: *The present situation is analogous to one that occurred in the 1930s.*
ANXIOUS	Mistakenly used to mean "eager."
	INCORRECT: *I'm so anxious to see my new grandson!*
	Anxious means "to be uneasy or apprehensive; worried."
	CORRECT: Sylvia grew anxious as her turn to speak drew closer.

BI- VS. SEMI- (WEEKLY, MONTHLY, ANNUAL)	The prefix *bi-* means "two or every two"; the prefix *semi-* means "half" or "twice." When those prefixes begin a word referring to a period of time, however, they can cause misunderstanding. *Bi-*, for example, has acquired a nonstandard meaning that is used frequently. Instead of meaning "twice," it now can also mean "every two." Thus *biweekly* can be interpreted as "twice a week" or "every two weeks." Confusing? Undoubtedly. In order to avoid confusion, it is often better to reword your message in order to make your meaning clear. For instance, if you mean every two weeks, say so, rather than using the words *biweekly* or *semimonthly*.

Here is a summary of usage:

Biweekly means "every two weeks." **NONSTANDARD:** "twice a week; *semiweekly*." *Bimonthly* means "every two months." **NONSTANDARD:** "twice a month; *semimonthly*." *Biyearly* means "every two years." **NONSTANDARD:** "twice a year; *semiyearly*."

But ... *Biannual* means "twice a year; *semiannual*." *Biennial* means "lasting two years; occurring every two years." *Semiweekly* means "twice a week." *Semimonthly* means "twice a month." *Semiannual* means "twice a year." |
| **COMPARE** | In formal usage, *compare* is used to note likenesses. *Contrast* is used to note differences.

INCORRECT: If you compare apples and oranges, you will find some striking differences between them.

In informal usage only, *compare with* may be used to note similarities or differences—but it is incorrect to use *compare to* in that same way. |
| **COMPENDIOUS** | Mistakenly used to mean "very lengthy; encyclopedic."

INCORRECT: Albertson's compendious, unabridged, Hungarian dictionary weighs over five pounds.

Compendious means "concise, terse, or abridged."

CORRECT: This short, compendious U.S. history devotes one paragraph to the dust bowl of the 1930s. |
| **CONSEQUENT** | Mistakenly used to mean "subsequent."

INCORRECT: After his first novel, consequent works were disappointing.

Consequent means "Following as a natural event or result of." |

Subsequent means "Following in time or order, succeeding."

CORRECT: A subsequent event is not necessarily a consequence of a preceding event.

DENOTE	Mistakenly used to mean "connote; to suggest or imply."
	INCORRECT: *To me, the word* home *denotes a place of rest, love, and comfort.*
	Denote means "to indicate; to refer to specifically."
	CORRECT: A fever may denote an infection.
DIFFUSE	Mistakenly used to mean "defuse; to reduce danger or tension."
	INCORRECT: He customarily used humor to diffuse tension in the workplace.
	Diffuse means "to disperse."
	CORRECT: Use this spray-atomizer to *diffuse* the scent throughout the room.
DOWNGRADE	Mistakenly used to mean "denigrate—to defame, slander, insult, or belittle."
	INCORRECT: *The candidate sought to downgrade his opponent's reputation.*
	Downgrade means "to lower the status or value of."
	CORRECT: The municipal bonds were *downgraded.*
DUE TO	Mistakenly used to introduce an adverbial phrase that gives the reason for or cause of the action of the main verb.
	INCORRECT: We were late due to construction delays on Route 44. Acceptable alternatives: *because of, through, on account of, owing to.*
	Due to functions as a predicate adjective after a linking verb (verb "to be") and means "because of."
	CORRECT: Her indecision was due to a lack of definite purpose.
ECONOMIC	Mistakenly used to mean "not wasteful; thrifty, economical."
	INCORRECT: Having an economic nature, he is always switching off lights.
	Economic means "relating to the economy or large-scale finances."
	CORRECT: What are the first signs of an economic recovery?

ENERVATE

Mistakenly used to mean "energize."

INCORRECT: I take a brisk walk before breakfast to enervate me and make me alert.

Enervate means "to drain of energy, to weaken."

CORRECT: The heat and humidity of the tropics combined to enervate us and rob us of initiative.

ENORMITY

Mistakenly used to mean "enormousness, immensity."

INCORRECT: We were overwhelmed by the enormity of the Colosseum.

Enormity means "outside moral boundaries, heinous on a huge scale, excessive wickedness."

CORRECT: The enormity of the regime's crimes were beyond belief.

ETC.

Mistakenly used to refer to people.

INCORRECT: The course is of benefit to writers, speakers, students, etc.

Etc. means "and so forth, and the rest." It is used at the end of a list of things, not of people.

CORRECT: Bring any kind of dessert, such as cheesecake, apple pie, English trifles, Bavarian cream, etc.

FLUKE

Mistakenly used to mean "a stroke of bad luck."

Fluke always refers to a stroke of good luck or a fortunate chance event. It originally referred to a lucky stroke in billiards.

GOURMAND

Mistakenly used to mean a gourmet, one who appreciates fine food and drink.

INCORRECT: You won't go wrong letting Herb choose the restaurant. He's a gourmand!

A *gourmand* is someone who eats to excess, a glutton.

CORRECT: It was repugnant to watch the gourmand stuff himself with food.

INFAMOUS

Mistakenly used to mean "famous."

INCORRECT: The highly esteemed actor rose from being a rodeo rider to an honored celebrity with an infamous reputation.

Infamous means "having a bad reputation, detestable."

CORRECT: The identity of the infamous serial killer Jack the Ripper remains unknown.

INGENUOUS

Mistakenly used to mean "intelligent, clever, ingenious."

INCORRECT: What a clever invention, and how ingenuous of you to have thought of it!

Ingenuous means "candid, naïve, not sophisticated."

CORRECT: The ingenuous young man did not realize that the frank expression of his opinion was not appropriate.

IRONIC

Mistakenly used to mean "an amusing coincidence."

INCORRECT: How ironic that we have the same birthday!

Ironic means "an outcome opposite from the expected outcome; an intended meaning opposite to the literal meaning."

CORRECT: How ironic that he spent his life trying to achieve fame, yet it was his death that made him famous.

LIMPID

Mistakenly used to mean "limp, frail."

INCORRECT: The limpid, wilted daffodils drooped loosely over the edge of the vase.

Limpid means "transparently clear; easily intelligible."

CORRECT: The pure and limpid stream has its source in the mountains.

LITERALLY

Mistakenly used to mean "practically."

INCORRECT: The children were literally bursting with anticipation and excitement.

Literally means "actually, without exaggeration."

CORRECT: He literally does not know how to boil an egg.

MITIGATE

Mistakenly used for *militate*, which means "to have an effect against, to counteract."

INCORRECT: The proposed amendment mitigates against free speech.

Mitigate means "to moderate; to make less bad.

CORRECT: The lawyer pleaded mitigating circumstances to reduce her client's sentence.

MORBID

Mistakenly used to mean "sad, unpleasant."

INCORRECT: His morbid disposition is his only companion.

Morbid means "diseased, unhealthy in body or mind."

CORRECT: He is mentally unstable and has a morbid fascination with death.

MUTE

Mistakenly used to mean "open to debate, debatable, as in 'a moot' point."

INCORRECT: Arguing about whether to go to the mountains or the beach is a mute point, since we can't afford to go on vacation.

Mute means "refraining from or unable to speak."

CORRECT: I couldn't hear the video because I had mistakenly hit the mute button.

NAVAL

Mistakenly used to mean "the depression in the middle of the abdomen of mammals where the umbilical cord was attached during gestation, belly button, navel."

INCORRECT: The belly dancer wore a sparkling jewel in her naval.

Naval means "of or pertaining to a navy."

CORRECT: This naval telescope collapses to fit in a sailor's pocket.

NEMESIS

Mistakenly used to mean merely "an enemy, a hostile person."

INCORRECT: I'm always tripping over that cat. She's my nemesis!

Nemesis is a much stronger word than *enemy*. It is "an avenging force." In classical mythology Nemesis was the goddess of retribution. She punished both excessive pride and wrongdoing and came to represent retributive justice or revenge. In sports, a *nemesis* is an unbeatable rival.

CORRECT: Superman's arch nemesis is Lex Luthor, just as Batman's is the Joker.

NONPLUSSED

Mistakenly used to mean "cool, calm, and collected."

INCORRECT: Nonplussed by his tirade, she calmly walked out the door and closed it quietly behind her.

Nonplussed means "perplexed, baffled, bewildered."

	CORRECT: Nonplussed by her remark, he wondered, "Whatever does she mean?"
ODIOUS	Mistakenly used to mean "detectable by smell, odorous, or odiferous."
	INCORRECT: I was repulsed by the odious smell of stale cigar smoke.
	Odious has no connection with the word *odor*. It means "hateful, abhorrent, offensive."
	CORRECT: With a sigh, he began the odious task of correcting exam papers.
OFFICIOUS	Mistakenly used to mean "like an officer."
	INCORRECT: He handled the task admirably, in an officious and commanding manner.
	Officious has nothing to do with the words *officer* or *official*. It means "aggressively nosy, meddlesome, excessively forward in offering service or advice."
	CORRECT: My landlord is an officious busybody who is always barging in with unwanted suggestions and offers of assistance.
PEACEABLE	Mistakenly used to mean "serene, calm, peaceful."
	INCORRECT: I love to retreat to this quiet, peaceable spot by the lake.
	Peaceable means "inclined to avoid strife; disposed toward peace."
	CORRECT: In one of Edward Hicks's Peaceable Kingdom paintings, William Penn is shown concluding a peaceable treaty with the Indians.
PENULTIMATE	Mistakenly used to mean "ultimate."
	INCORRECT: This resort spa is absolutely fabulous, the penultimate in luxury!
	Penultimate means "the next to last."
	CORRECT: This is the fourth, or penultimate, concert in the series of five, which will conclude on January 25.
PERUSE	Mistakenly used to mean "to look over casually; to glance over quickly."
	INCORRECT: *I perused the book quickly and decided it wasn't for me.*
	Peruse means "to read or examine thoroughly, with great care."

CORRECT: Peruse this report carefully to ensure there are no ambiguous statements or inaccuracies.

PLETHORA	Mistakenly used to mean "a lot, many."

INCORRECT: The newly married couple was welcomed by a plethora of well-wishers.

Plethora means "overabundance, an excess." It often carries a negative connotation.

CORRECT: The bill needs to pass through a plethora of committees and subcommittees before being considered for a vote.

PRACTICABLE	Mistakenly used to mean "relating to practice rather than theory, practical."

INCORRECT: The book is a straightforward, practicable guide to finding an apartment in New York City.

Practicable means "possible, capable of being done or used."

CORRECT: Although constructing a bridge over the Strait of Messina may be practicable, the immense cost involved probably makes it impractical.

PRECEDENCE	Mistakenly used to mean "an act or instance that may be used to judge subsequent incidences; a precedent."

INCORRECT: This law decision might set a dangerous precedence.

Precedence means "to go before; take priority."

CORRECT: Those arriving first will be given precedence for seating.

PRISTINE	Mistakenly used to mean "spotless; as good as new."

INCORRECT: The carpet was spotless, a pristine white.

Pristine means "pertaining to the earliest time or condition; in a state virtually unchanged from the original."

CORRECT: The gold coins they recovered were pristine, in newly minted condition.

PROGENITOR	Mistakenly used to mean "inventor."

INCORRECT: Thomas A. Edison was the progenitor of the lightbulb.

Progenitor means "direct ancestor."

CORRECT: President John Adams was the progenitor of a distinguished family, including his son President John Quincy Adams.

QUAY

Mistakenly used to mean "an offshore island, a key."

INCORRECT: We beached our boat on an uninhabited quay about five miles from the mainland.

Quay (pronounced like *key*) means "a wharf or landing place built parallel to a waterway to unload ships."

CORRECT: We walked down the wide cement quay, which was alongside the riverbank.

RANDOM

Mistakenly used to mean "spontaneous; someone living in an irregular and unrestrained way."

INCORRECT: She is an impulsive, random person.

Random means "having no specific pattern; chance, arbitrary."

CORRECT: The winning ticket number will be selected at random from all the tickets sold.

REDUNDANT

Mistakenly used to mean "useless or unable to perform or function."

INCORRECT: When is Riley going to admit that he's redundant, that it's time for him to retire?"

Redundant means "superfluous; needlessly repetitive."

CORRECT: In the phrase "last will and testament," the word *testament* is redundant because it is repetitious.

RESTIVE

Mistakenly used to mean "restful, conducive to rest."

INCORRECT: Unfortunately, our vacation was not restive because of the noisy children in the next room.

Restive means "impatient, stubborn; restless, agitated."

CORRECT: The audience grew restive waiting for the rock concert to start.

RETICENT

Mistakenly used to mean "reluctant."

INCORRECT: He is reticent to commit himself to a relationship.

Reticent means "be silent, reserved, taciturn."

CORRECT: He is never reticent when asked to express his opinion of rap music.

SEASONABLE	Mistakenly used to mean "relating to or dependent on a season, seasonal." **INCORRECT:** Jobs in the amusement park are seasonable. *Seasonable* means "timely, appropriate to the season." **CORRECT:** This cool weather will be gone by Wednesday and will become more seasonable for July.
TANTAMOUNT	Mistakenly used to mean "best, the top, paramount." **INCORRECT:** This committee's tantamount concern is to arrive at the truth. *Tantamount* means "equal to in effect or value." **CORRECT:** To say you don't recall what the committee discussed and concluded is tantamount to admitting your incompetence.
UNDO	Mistakenly used to mean "excessive, not just, undue." **INCORRECT:** If your job causes undo stress, quit! *Undo* means "to reverse or erase; to untie or unstrap." **CORRECT:** If only I could undo the injury I have done you!
VERSE	In formal usage, *verse* is mistakenly used to mean "a poem or stanza (division) of a poem." **INCORRECT:** I finally memorized that entire verse on Hiawatha by Longfellow. *Verse* means "a line of poetry." **CORRECT:** The poem consists of three stanzas, with four verses in each stanza.
WRONGFUL	Mistakenly used as a synonym for wrong. **INCORRECT:** We made a wrongful turn and got lost. *Wrongful* means "unjust, unfair; not sanctioned by law." **CORRECT:** Did circumstantial evidence lead to her wrongful conviction for the crime?

05
PURGE 25 NO-NO'S FROM YOUR SPEECH & WRITING

Sir, it is not so much to be lamented that Old England is lost, as that the Scotch [sic] have found it.

—SAMUEL JOHNSON

No-no's are mistakes. They occur so often that in many cases they have come to sound and look correct. It's easy to use them yourself, but don't be misled. Those in the know frown on such words and phrases because they are incorrect either grammatically or lexically (relating to vocabulary).

No-no's include nonexistent words (e.g., *alright*), incorrect idiomatic expressions (e.g., *could care less*), incorrect idiomatic use of prepositions (e.g., *could of*), nonstandard usage or meanings (e.g., *ignorant* to mean "rude"), and words with built-in redundancies (e.g., *reiterate*). I selected the no-no's in this chapter because they are common grammatical and lexical errors and are frequently listed in style guides and usage manuals. I have listed them in a table to make them easy to access.

Begin by scanning the entries on the following pages to discover which you need to study. Undoubtedly, you will recognize some entries as known errors, but others may give you pause: "Is that an error? I didn't realize that." Since the list is a manageable size, a brief scan will quickly tell you what you need to learn. All of the errors listed occur frequently, both in speech and writing.

Be one of the few who knows your *no-no's* and refuses to use them. Show your superior word savvy. Purge the following offenders from your speech and your writing.

1. ALOT	Not a word. Instead, use two separate words: *a lot*. *A lot* means "a large number or amount; to a great degree or extent."
	CORRECT: A lot of people write the words *a lot* incorrectly as one word.
2. ALRIGHT	Not a word. Write it as two words: *all right*. Because *all right* is commonly spoken as one word, it is mistakenly written that way, as well. *All right* means "very well, okay, without a doubt."
	CORRECT: After the storm, we checked the property to make sure everything was all right.
3. ANYWAYS	*Anyways* was an acceptable word in Middle English, but it has outlived its usefulness and acceptability. Avoid *anyways* and replace it with *anyway*. *Anyway* is an adverb, and adverbs are plural. Thus it cannot end in the *s*-plural.
	Anyway means "regardless, in any event, in any manner whatever, nevertheless."
	CORRECT: I know I probably won't win, but I intend to enter the contest anyway.
4. BEG THE QUESTION	This expression is mistakenly used to mean "raise the question or bring up the question."
	INCORRECT: The fact that you never grade my excellent essays above a C begs the question, why do you grade me unfairly?
	To *beg the question* means to present as true or take for granted a premise that needs proof—assuming as true what needs to be proved (otherwise known as a "circular argument").
	CORRECT: You beg the question by stating I grade you unfairly because I never grade your excellent essays above a C. Are your essays excellent? That is the question you should be asking.
5. BURSTED	This is an incorrect form of the verb *to burst* (whose principal parts are: *burst, burst, burst.*) In other words, there is no such word as *bursted*. Use *burst* instead.

INCORRECT: The child winced as the balloon bursted.

CORRECT: The child winced as the balloon burst.

6. BY THE POWER INVESTED IN ME

The correct phrase is *By the power vested in me*. *Invested* usually refers to financial transactions. *Vested* means "bestowed on; conferred on."

INCORRECT: By the power invested in me by the State of New Jersey ...

CORRECT: By the power vested in me by the State of New Jersey ...

7. COULD CARE LESS

The correct phrase is *could not care less* or *couldn't care less*.

INCORRECT: *I could care less about ice hockey*. This is illogical. It means that the speaker cares about ice hockey but possibly could care less about it.

CORRECT: I am not at all interested in ice hockey and couldn't care less about it.

8. COULD OF

The correct expression is *could have*, not *could of*.

INCORRECT: I could of danced all night!

CORRECT: I could have danced all night.

9. DILIGENCY

Not a word. Instead, use *diligence*.

INCORRECT: He applied himself to the task with diligency.

Diligence means "persistent effort; long, steady application to work or study."

CORRECT: He applied himself to the task with diligence.

10. ESCAPE GOAT

The correct word is *scapegoat*. Its origin traces back to an ancient rite on the Hebrew Day of Atonement when the high priest lay the sins of the people on the head of a goat. The goat was then taken into the wilderness to carry away the sins of the people. (Perhaps the original word did mean "escape goat," since the goat escaped into the wilderness and also escaped being sacrificed.)

Scapegoat means a person, often innocent, on whom blame is heaped or punishment inflicted for something someone else has done. In the vernacular, a *scapegoat* is a "fall guy."

CORRECT: Although innocent, he became the scapegoat because they needed someone to blame.

11. FASTLY

Not a word. The correct word is *fast,* which is used both as an adjective and adverb.

INCORRECT: With the holidays fastly approaching, I'd better start shopping.

CORRECT: With the holidays fast approaching, I'd better start shopping.

12. FINAL ULTIMATUM

This phrase is redundant since *ultimatum* encompasses the meaning "final." Use *ultimatum* by itself, without a modifier. *Ultimatum* means "a final statement of terms; one's last word on a subject."

CORRECT: Rejection of our ultimatum may lead to the severing of diplomatic relations.

13. FOR ALL INTENSIVE PURPOSES

The correct phrase is *for all intents and purposes.*

For all intents and purposes means "for all practical purposes; in effect."

CORRECT: These unsold items from our garage sale are, for all intents and purposes, useless.

14. HEART-WRENCHING

Not a word. It may have originated by mistakenly connecting it to the similar word *gut-wrenching.* The correct word is *heartrending. Heartrending* means, "inciting anguish, arousing deep sympathy; extremely moving."

CORRECT: The Derby opened with a heartrending rendition of "My Old Kentucky Home."

15. HONE IN ON

The correct phrase is *home in on. Home in on* means "to aim at a target" (as a homing pigeon aims at its home). In contrast, *to hone* means "to sharpen" (as you would *hone* a blade to sharpen it).

CORRECT: Police are homing in on the robbery suspect.

16. IGNORANT

Mistakenly used to mean "rude" rather than "uneducated, not knowledgeable."

CORRECT: Although initially ignorant of official protocol, she learned quickly.

17. IRREGARDLESS

Not a standard word. Instead, use *regardless. Regardless* means "in spite of; without regard for."

CORRECT: I must have that ring regardless of its cost.

18. NAUSEOUS	Mistakenly used to mean nauseated.
	INCORRECT: I feel nauseous.
	CORRECT: I feel nauseated.
	Nauseous means "causing or able to cause nausea."
	CORRECT: The nauseous odor made me feel sick.
19. ORIENTATED	The correct word is *oriented*. *Oriented* means "aligned in position with reference to another point."
	CORRECT: The architect oriented the entrance to face south.
20. QUICKER	There is *quick and quickly*, but no such word as *quicker*. Instead, use *faster*.
21. REITERATE	Avoid using this word. Purists object to it on the grounds that it is redundant. Since *iterate* means "to say again, to repeat," the *re* prefix, meaning "again" is a redundancy.
22. REOCCURRENCE	Not a word. Instead, use *recurrence*. *Recurrence* means "to *occur again*; to return to one's memory."
	CORRECT: Fortunately, once the leak was fixed, there was no recurrence of the problem.
23. SCOTCH	Mistakenly used as an adjective to refer to a person or object from Scotland.
	INCORRECT: Angus MacPherson is Scotch.
	Use the following words to refer to people from Scotland: *Scot, Scots, Scotsman, Scottish*.
	CORRECT: Angus MacPherson is a Scot (or Scotsman).
24. STATUE OF LIMITATIONS	The correct phrase is *statute of limitations*. A *statute of limitations* prescribes the time period in which legal action can take place.
25. SUPPOSE TO	Particularly in speech, *suppose to* is incorrectly used for *supposed to*.
	INCORRECT: I know I'm suppose to exercise.
	Supposed to means that something should be done, but often it isn't. *Suppose* (used without to) means "imagine or expect."
	CORRECT: I know I'm supposed to exercise, and I suppose I'll be sorry if I don't.

06

USE TRICKY SINGULARS & PLURALS WITH ASSURANCE

Remember: Y'all is singular. All y'all is plural.
All y'all's is plural possessive.

—KINKY FRIEDMAN

Often making a word plural is as simple as adding an *-s* or *-es*, but when you're dealing with plurals of foreign words, compound nouns, proper names, and number and letters, it can get tricky. This chapter will give you the know-how you need to avoid errors.

FOREIGN PLURALS

English words derived from other languages often have irregular plural forms, although the trend is to Anglicize such words and use the regular *–s* plural ending. Many scientific terms are derived from Latin or Greek and retain their original endings when used by professionals in the sciences, even though they may be Anglicized in common usage.

Nouns that were "borrowed" from a foreign language often retain their foreign spellings for their plurals. Others have been Anglicized and form plurals by adding *–s* or *-es*. Still others have two plurals—an Anglicized plural as well as the original foreign plural. When in doubt about whether or not it is acceptable to use the Anglicized rather the foreign plural, check a dictionary to see which spelling is preferable. In *Merriam Webster's Collegiate Dictionary* (the standard spelling reference for many style guides), the first spelling listed is the preferred spelling for nouns that have two plurals.

Here are some general guidelines on how to form foreign plurals:

a → ae   If the noun ends in *a*, change *a* to *ae*: *alumna/alumnae*.

us → i   If the noun ends in *us*, change *us* to *i*: *alumnus/alumni*.

is → es   If the noun ends in *is*, change *is* to *es*: *crisis/crises*.

on → a   If the noun ends in *on*, change *on* to *a*: *phenomenon/phenomena*.

um → a   If the noun ends in *um*, change *um* to *a*: *bacterium/bacteria*.

ix/ex → es   If the noun ends in *ix* or *ex*, change *ix* or *ex* to *es*: *index/indices*. (The Anglicized version of nouns ending in *ix* or *ex* adds *es* to the singular form. Anglicized versions usually are acceptable except in scientific or technical writing: *appendixes, indexes, vertexes, vortexes, matrixes*. Note that *indexes* is used when referring to books; *indices* is used in mathematics.)

o → i   If the word ends in *o*, change the *o* to *i*: *libretto/libretti*; *tempo/tempi*; *virtuoso/virtuosi*; *graffito/graffiti*. (Anglicized plurals add *s*: *librettos, tempos, virtuosos*.)

eau → eaux   If the word ends in *eau*, change the *eau* to *eaux*. The *x* is pronounced *z*: *château/châteaux*; *gâteau/gâteaux*; *plateau/plateaux*; *trousseau/trousseaux*. (Anglicized plurals add *s*: *plateaus, trousseaus*.)

See the following table for examples of singular and plural forms of nouns derived from foreign languages. When two plurals are listed, the preferred plural (according to *Webster's*) is listed first.

SINGULAR	PLURAL
addendum	addenda
alga	algae
adieu	adieus or adieux

alumna (female)	alumnae (female)
alumnus (male)	alumni (male)
analysis	analyses
antenna	antennae or antennas
appendix	appendices or appendixes
automaton	automatons
axis	axes
bacterium	bacteria
basis	bases
beau	beaux or beaus
bureau	bureaus or bureaux
cactus	cacti or cactuses
chateau	chateaux or chateaus
cherub	cherubim or cherubs
concerto	concerti or concertos
corpus	corpora
cortex	cortices or cortexes
crisis	crises
criterion	criteria
curriculum	curricula or curriculums
datum	data
diagnosis	diagnoses
dogma	dogmas or dogmata
ellipsis	ellipses
emphasis	emphases
encyclopedia	encyclopedias
erratum	errata
focus	focuses or foci
formula	formulae or formulas

forum	forums or forma
fungus	fungi or funguses
gâteau	gâteaux
genus	genera
hippopotamus	hippopotamuses or hippopotami
honorarium	honoraria or honorariums
hypothesis	hypotheses
index	indices or indexes
kibbutz	kibbutzim
larva	larvae
locus	loci
matrix	matrices or matrixes
matzo	matzoth or matzos
maximum	maxima or maximums
medium or media (Media is now often treated as a singular mass noun.)	media
memorandum	memorandums or memoranda
millennium	millennia or millenniums
minimum	minima or minimums
minutia	minutiae
mitzvah	mitzvoth or mitzvahs
nucleus	nuclei or nucleuses
octopus	octopuses or octopi
parenthesis	parentheses
persona	personae or personas
phenomenon	phenomena
plateau	plateaus or plateaux
platypus	platypuses
radius	radii or radiuses

referendum	referenda, referendums
schema	schemata
seraph	seraphim or seraphs
stadium	stadia, stadiums
stigma	stigmata or stigmas
stimulus	stimuli
stoma	stomata or stomas
stratum	strata
syllabus	syllabuses or syllabi
symposium	symposia or symposiums
synopsis	synopses
synthesis	syntheses
tableau	tableaux or tableaus
testis	testes
thesis	theses
trousseau	trousseaux or trousseaus
ultimatum	ultimatums or ultimata
vertebra	vertebrae or vertebras
vertex	vertices or vertexes
virus	viruses
vortex	vortices or vortexes

PLURALS OF COMPOUND NOUNS

Plurals of compound nouns can be tricky. Which of the words in the compound is made plural? Or, are both words made plural? Such are the pesky questions about plural compounds that annoy writers. Guidelines for forming plural compounds are given below. Some tricky plurals are listed in *Webster's*, such as *fathers-in-law*, *brothers-in-law*, *coups d'état*, *chefs d'oeuvre*, and *courts-martial*.

1. COMPOUNDS WRITTEN AS ONE WORD. Make the final word of the compound plural, usually by adding *s* or *es* :

> armful/armfuls, birthday/birthdays, bookshelf/bookshelves, cupful/cupfuls, eyelash/eyelashes, flashback/flashbacks, foothold/footholds, forefoot/forefeet, grandchild/grandchildren, handful/handfuls, hatbox/hatboxes, mousetrap/mousetraps, photocopy/photocopies, printout/printouts, strawberry/strawberries, teaspoonful/teaspoonfuls, toothbrush/toothbrushes, wineglass/wineglasses.

2. COMPOUNDS FORMED BY A NOUN AND ONE OR MORE MODIFIERS. Make the noun plural. The noun is the chief element in the compound.

> account payable/accounts payable, adjutant general/adjutants general, aide-de-camp/aides-de-camp, assistant attorney general/assistant attorneys general, assistant attorney/assistant attorneys, assistant corporation counsel/assistant corporation counsels, attorney general/attorneys general, bill of lading/bills of lading, child wife/child wives, coup d'état/coups d'état, court martial/courts martial, daughter-in-law/daughters-in-law, deputy chief of staff/deputy chiefs of staff, deputy sheriff/deputy sheriffs, editor-in-chief/editors-in-chief, history major/history majors, leave of absence/leaves of absence, letter of credit/letters of credit, lieutenant colonel/lieutenant colonels, looker-on/lookers-on, major general/major generals, man-of-war/men-of-war, passerby/passersby, postmaster general/postmasters general, president-elect/presidents-elect, runner-up/runners-up, secretary general/secretaries general, senator-elect/senators-elect, sergeant major/sergeants major, surgeon general/surgeons general.

PLURALS OF PROPER NAMES, NUMBERS, AND LETTERS

Most names (of individuals, families, products, and companies) are made plural by adding *s* or *es.* (Don't use an apostrophe *-s* to make a name plural.)

the Bachs	the Browns	the Ricardos
the Carsons	the Mugfords	the Nickells
the IBMs	the Intels	the Whites

If the name ends in *ch, s, z, x,* or *sh,* add *es* to form the plural. (But omit the *es* if it would make the plural awkward to pronounce: e.g., *Bridges,* not *Bridgeses.*)

| the Marches | the Jameses | the Katzes |
| the Maddoxes | the Nashes | the Welshes |

If the name ends in *y, add* s to form the plural.

| the Kennedys | the two Marys | the McCarthys |
| the Raffertys | the two Kansas Citys (*Cities* would be misleading) |

When a numeral is used as a word, add *s to form the plural.*

| the 1920s | size 9s | temperatures in the 90s |

When a number is expressed as a word, add *s* or *es to form the plural.*

| ones | twenty-fives | fifties | sixes |

For capital letters and abbreviations consisting of capital letters add *s* to form the plural.

| IQs | three Rs | M.D.s | Ph.D.s | ABCs |

For letters that are not capitalized, form the plural by adding apostrophe -*s.* This is done to prevent misreading. (Some style guides add apostrophe -*s* to capitalized nouns, as well.)

| o's | p's and q's | c.o.d.'s | dot your i's |

QUIZ: TRICKY SINGULARS & PLURALS

Rewrite the sentences below to practice changing singulars to plurals. Change each noun in parentheses to its correct plural form. (Some nouns have alternate plurals. In such cases, either plural is correct.) Answers are on page 209.

1. The entertainment, provided by (*alumnus*) and (*alumna*), consisted of two (*concerto*) for oboe and three short (*tableau*) in which the performers took on the (*persona*) of (*cherub*) and (*seraph*).

2. After multiple (*analysis*) of (*datum*) according to agreed-on (*criterion*), we were able to reject (*hypothesis*) whose (*basis*) rested on defective (*schema*).

3. If you could examine the (*corpus*) of the following life forms, which could contain all three of these structures—cerebral (*cortex*), (*testis*), and (*vertebra*): (*alga*), (*bacterium*), (*virus*), (*fungus*), (*hippopotamus*), (*larva*), (*octopus*), and (*platypus*)?

4. After sharing (*gâteau*) and (*matzo*) with their former (*beau*), Adele and Jeannine said their (*adieu*) and bravely traversed the river's raging (*vortex*) to return to their respective (*château*) on the (*vertex*) of adjoining mountains, where they contemplated their (*trousseau*), stored in massive mahogany (*bureau*).

5. The (*Burgess*), who delighted in (*minutia*), sought to improve their (*IQ*) by finding errors in (*encyclopedia*), recording them in (*memorandum*), and submitting them to publishers' (*editor-in-chief*) as (*erratum*)—or to the (*medium*), if publishers made the mistake of ignoring them.

07
SOME SURPRISING WAYS ERRORS OCCUR

As long as the world is turning and spinning, we're gonna be dizzy and we're gonna make mistakes.

—MEL BROOKS

Knowing the right word is, of course, the best way to prevent errors; but errors still occur, even when you know the right word. Learning how and when these errors occur will help you prevent and correct them.

Wrong-word errors are not only embarrassing but costly, as publisher Penguin Books Australia can attest. In 2010, the publisher was forced to reprint seven thousand copies of the cookbook *Pasta Bible* because it called for adding "salt and freshly ground black people" (instead of black pepper) to a recipe for tagliatelle with sardines and prosciutto. Oops! That slip cost the publisher some $20,000 to correct. How could such a slipup happen?

HOW TYPOS OCCUR

Curiously, being adept at typing can cause you to make typos. This is how it happens. Since you are an adept typist, you type automatically, not word by word. Your mind moves ahead of your fingers—usually by at least several words. It is easy to mistakenly type the word you are thinking of instead of the next word to be typed.

Other typos occur by absentmindedly typing the wrong word of a pair of easily confused words. As noted in chapter 1 of this book, English contains numerous examples of confusing word pairs and trios, making it remarkably easy to type the wrong word. How *humidifying!*

Finally, some typos do occur by striking the wrong letter on the keyboard or, in printed copy, because the printer (not the author) made an error.

Was the typo in the recipe caused by a typing error? Probably not. It is unlikely that the writer was thinking ahead to the word *people* when typing a recipe. Nor is *people* a word commonly confused with *pepper.* Likewise, *pepper* could not be transformed to *people* by striking the wrong key on the keyboard. What might have happened is that the substitution of *people* for *pepper* was made by a computerized spell-check program, and the error was not caught by a proofreader.

ERRORS INITIATED BY SPELL-CHECKERS

How can a spell-checker cause wrong-word errors? Many spell-check programs have an auto-correct feature. When that feature is turned on and you misspell a word, the program automatically "corrects" it by replacing the misspelled word with the word that is the best choice, statistically speaking. But that "correct" word, although spelled correctly, is often the wrong word—not the word you intended to write. The only way to spot and correct such spell-checker errors is through careful proofreading.

Contractions are particularly troublesome for spell-checkers. Spell-checkers want to change *it's* to *its* and *you're* to *your,* for example. Be alert for such problems when proofreading.

A wrong-word error may also result from blindly following a spell-checker's suggestion. An increasingly frequent error, for example, is *of coarse* for *of course.* In such a case, the writer misspells *course.* Spell-check picks up the misspelling and offers suggested spellings. The writer chooses *coarse* and doesn't bother to look it up because it looks right. It looks right because it is a word the writer has seen before. Unfortunately, it is the wrong word.

Finally, beware of thoughtlessly adding misspelled words to your spell-checker's dictionary. When your spell-check spots a word it does not recognize, it will ask you if you want to add it to the dictionary. If you click on "yes" without thinking and the word is misspelled, that misspelling will from then on be recognized as "correct."

ERRORS CAUSED BY USE OF A COMPUTERIZED THESAURUS

In addition to their explicit meaning, many words carry connotations—positive or negative shades of meaning. Thus while the adjectives *slender, svelte, slim, lean, scrawny, bony, gaunt,* and *spindly* can all be used to denote a person who is thin, the first four adjectives carry positive connotations; the last four carry negative connotations. If you use a computerized thesaurus feature to find synonyms, make sure you are well-acquainted with any synonym you choose, or if not, look it up in a dictionary. Otherwise you may unknowingly choose a word that doesn't suit what you're trying to say. Suppose, for example, you want a synonym for *famous* and look it up in your computer's thesaurus feature. One of the synonyms you find is *notorious.* You have seen that adjective used before, possibly in reference to celebrities, and you like it. You decide it sounds noble, distinguished. But if you choose it to describe a famous person you admire, you will have chosen the wrong word. *Notorious* connotes someone who has achieved fame for the wrong reasons—someone who is disreputable, dishonorable, tarnished, and *infamous*—the very opposite of the meaning you want to convey.

ERRORS CAUSED BY DISREGARDING AUDIENCE

According to Naomi Baron, professor of linguistics and language at American University, writing today is changing both because our society is "increasingly less formal" and because of the widespread influence of digital writing tools and online communication. She says that online communication tends to be sloppier than traditional forms of writing and that writing in general is becoming more informal and speechlike. There does seem to be some resistance to editing what is written online. That would account for some of the sloppiness of online communication. Perhaps this is due in part to social support for the idea that it is okay to write or say whatever you think in whatever language or form you wish to express yourself. That's what creativity is all about, isn't it? Is it really necessary to edit online communication?

Editing does take time, and one thing about online communication is that it's fast. Online writing is usually done quickly. Because communications can be dispatched so rapidly—just click and send—there is a social pressure for us to compose and send without pondering our communication or even reading it over. Indeed, with instant messaging, there is someone sitting there waiting while we hastily type a reply. Writing in a hurry is a realistic description of how writing online affects writing.

How does all of this apply to wrong-word errors? It has to do with your audience, on who will read your writing. Where word choice is concerned it is absolutely essential to keep your audience in mind as you write, and—depending on your audience—it may be essential to edit your writing for word choice, as well. For example, when you're writing to a friend, it may be perfectly appropriate to include colloquialisms, slang, emoticons, and Textese (e.g., IDK to mean "I don't know"). But those same words would fall into the "wrong word" category if you included them in an e-mail to a prospective employer or writing professor. A "right word" in one context may be the "wrong word" in another.

Buzzwords (which we'll discuss in chapter 9) are a prime example of tailoring your wording to your audience. To explain a marketing project to a co-worker, buzzwords will likely be effective; but in explaining it to your spouse, buzzwords may be the wrong words.

It all depends on the relationship you have with the recipient and on having an understanding of the recipient's prior knowledge of and thoughts on the subject. Thus keep your audience in mind when you write or speak. Watch your words, suit your words to your audience—and you will use the right words every time.

08
How to Catch
Wrong-Word Errors

*I was working on the proof of one of my poems all morning,
and took out a comma. In the afternoon I put it back again.*

—Oscar Wilde

Whether through confusion or carelessness, wrong-word errors happen. They will happen to you as they do to every writer, no matter how meticulous, how careful. As was demonstrated in previous chapters, checking for wrong-word errors is not a job you can hand over to your spell-checker or grammar checker. Yet, checking for wrong-word errors is absolutely essential. If not caught, such errors sink your credibility and sabotage your success. In the final analysis, then, it is up to you to catch and correct wrong-word errors through careful proofreading.

Fortunately, proofreading skills are not innate. They can be learned, developed, and improved. What is the best source for information on how to proofread? Logically, the best guidance it that obtained from professional proofreaders, from those who have spent years developing tricks and techniques to perfect their proofreading skills. The section that follows offers professional proofreaders' tips, procedures, and techniques on how to proofread. Some of these tips are particularly useful in proofreading for wrong-word errors, such as reading backwards and concentrating on reading one word at a time. The tips are not listed in a particular order. Proofreaders agree, however, that running a spell-check/grammar check should be your first step.

HOW TO PROOFREAD LIKE A PROFESSIONAL

Follow the tips below from professional proofreaders to be confident that you have taken the necessary steps to error-proof your writing

- **RUN SPELL-CHECK/GRAMMAR CHECK.** Run your computerized spell-check/grammar-check programs, but don't depend on them to catch all the errors. Moreover, consider carefully any suggestion they offer before accepting it and making the requested change. Don't be intimidated by your editing programs and blindly accept every changed word or spelling they suggest. If you are not positive a suggested change is correct, look it up in a dictionary.

- **ALLOW SOME TIME TO ELAPSE BETWEEN WRITING AND PROOF-READING.** When you proofread immediately after writing, your brain remembers what you just wrote and automatically makes corrections. Such mental corrections are useless. It's what's on paper that counts. Follow the advice of the National Secretaries Association: *Proofread tomorrow what you worked on today.*

- **CONTROL YOUR ENVIRONMENT.** Choose a quiet time to proofread and a quiet room. You need to be able to concentrate without interruption. Shut the door. Turn off your phone's ring tone. Make sure you can see without eyestrain, adjusting the lighting as necessary.

- **PROOFREAD WHEN YOU ARE MENTALLY ALERT.** You won't spot errors if you are mentally or physically exhausted. Proofreading at such times will be wasted effort—or worse. You might overlook a crucial, glaring mistake. If possible, proofread later when you've revived. Or take an exercise break or a brisk walk in the great outdoors.

- **READ SLOWLY AND OUT LOUD, IF POSSIBLE.** If you can't read aloud without disturbing others, subvocalize; that is, read softly to yourself. Use proper intonation as you read. It will help you spot faulty sentence construction, incorrect punctuation, and grammatical errors.

- **CONCENTRATE ON READING ONE WORD AT A TIME.** As you read aloud, make an effort to concentrate on each individual word and ask yourself if it is the right word. Be aware that we all have a tendency to mentally fill in missing letters we don't see on the page.

- **READ BACKWARDS.** Start at the end of your document and read it backwards word by word. This little trick forces you to read one word at a time because you aren't distracted by content.

- **READ WITH A DOUBT IN YOUR MIND.** Assume that each word is incorrect. Be skeptical. This will help you read word by word without being distracted by the meaning of what you are reading.

- **BE ON THE ALERT FOR YOUR MOST COMMON MISTAKES.** Most of us have certain "pet mistakes" we make repeatedly. Perhaps you frequently confuse a word pair or write *alot* for *a lot*. It's helpful to make a list of your most common mistakes and to check for them specifically.

- **PROOFREAD LINE BY LINE.** Read methodically line by line. Use a ruler to guide your eyes so you don't miss a line.

- **DON'T PROOFREAD ON THE COMPUTER SCREEN.** It is hard to spot errors on the computer screen. Print out the document and proofread the hard copy. If you do decide to proofread on-screen, print out a hard copy of the corrected document and proofread that as well for one final check. Most likely you will catch some errors on the screen and some on paper.

- **PROOFREAD THE ENTIRE DOCUMENT.** Don't skip titles and headings. Surprisingly, major typos often occur in headings and titles—even the titles of books! There is a tendency to skip over headings and get to the "real reading." Don't fall victim to this trap. Imagine your embarrassment if a wrong word appears in your document's title or in a boldface heading.

- **PROOFREAD MORE THAN ONCE AND FOR SPECIAL PURPOSES.** Proofread once for misspellings, another time for wrong-word errors, another for punctuation errors, for example.

- **HAVE SOMEONE ELSE PROOFREAD YOUR WORK.** Even if you are superb at spotting other writer's errors, recognize that it is very difficult to spot your own. Because you are so familiar with your writing and can almost recite parts of it by heart, you will have a natural tendency to scan what you have written and miss errors.

QUIZ: PROOFREADING FOR WRONG WORDS

Try your hand at proofreading to find wrong words. The following selection is chock-full of words that are frequently confused. How many can you catch and correct? (Check your answers on page 209)

Herd in a Bar

"What ales you, Harry? Why sit crying in you're bier? Yore pail, to. Your in pane, no?"

"Eye, George. I feel offal. Its really effected me. Its to hard too bare. I aired. I admit it. Its awl my fault. First of all, Ellie desserted me—left me at the alter, sow too speak. But theirs alot moor to it then that."

"Why knot tell me awl about it? Lets get down to brass tax."

"Tacks! That's just it, George. That's when it awl started. I've bin a full. I blue it. I cheated on my income tacks. I aught not to have done it. I lost my scents. Now Ellie nose it two. And now their coming after me."

"Dam! Not that, Harry! Not the IRS?"

"The very same. The Infernal Revenue Service. Theirs only won answer four me now, George. Boos!"

"Rite on, Harry. Aisle drink too that! Butt put your cache away. This Bud's on me, buddy!"

09

Talk the Talk: Keeping Abreast of Buzzwords

Buzzwords, keywords, business-speak, corporate-speak techno-jargon, or techno-speak—whatever the current colloquialisms and clichés of your workplace, you need to know what they are and stay on top of them. If success is your aim, you need to keep abreast of the buzzwords in your field. Not only do you need to walk the walk, you need to talk the talk (or at the least, be conversant in it).

Although buzzwords strike some as jarring, irritating, trivial, and trite, they do have their legitimate uses and their legitimate users. When used by the uninformed to convey an impression of being on the cutting edge, they instead label the user as ignorant and pretentious. But when used by those who are savvy and know what they actually mean, buzz-words can increase the clarity, precision, and impact of speech or writing. They can capture an image or difficult concept in a single word—"simplify the complex," as Mike Myatt put it. He goes on to say:

I have found that business-speak can be particularly beneficial in using just a few words to explain situations, scenarios, processes, trends, attitudes, and any number of other ethereal and esoteric concepts that might have otherwise have needed several sentences and paragraphs to describe. ... A person could either take several minutes to explain the evolution of technologies, mediums, shift in content paradigms, and engagement practices and market dynamics that came together to make the Internet a more valuable and efficient space, or they could just utilize "social media" as a descriptive aid to make the connection. The latter is much more efficient than the former.

Be on the alert for buzzwords in the workplace. When you encounter a new buzzword, think about who is using it and whether or not it enhances communication. Is its meaning clear? Is it a catchy, more concise way of expressing a concept that would take more words, more explanation to convey in plain English? If so, adopt it. If not, don't.

Recognize the value of the judicious use of buzzwords to consolidate your position as an insider, demonstrate that you know the terminology of your field, and show that you can speak its language fluently. An effective use of buzzwords demonstrates your word savvy.

Caution: Before using the latest catchy buzzword or phrase de jour, make sure you know what it really means. If you don't know, don't use it. Using a buzzword incorrectly is far worse than not using it at all. At the least, you risk being misunderstood, at the worst, embarrassed when you realize it is evident to others that you used the word for effect and do not really understand its meaning.

BUZZWORDS, OR KEYWORDS, IN RÉSUMÉS

It is especially important to be knowledgeable about buzzwords when you are looking for a job and preparing your résumé. This is because technology is playing an increasingly important role in the hiring process. Employers are using scanning software to screen résumés. Scanners screen thousands of résumés, looking specifically for a prioritized set of buzzwords, or *keywords*, as they are referred to in résumés. You can be sure that a résumé posted on a job site such as Monster.com or Headhunter.net will be screened in this way. But it is not just online résumés that will be scanned. Now, when most employers are swamped with applicants, even small companies scan résumés into computers and use scanning software to scan for their prioritized list of keywords. Scanning software has come a long way. Earlier software didn't recognize text in italics, boldface, special fonts, or bulleted text. Keywords were usually positioned in a summary at the head of the résumé to ensure they would be scanned. That is no longer necessary. Now they may be scattered throughout the document. This means that you can prepare a visually attractive, well-formatted résumé with keywords placed where they logically belong—a résumé that will stand out after it passes the first scanning and is selected for review by human eyes.

The Importance of Using the Right Keywords

If you want your résumé to pass the first screening and land in the list of possible candidates, you must include the most important (or a large number) of keywords on the employer's list. Résumés are ranked according to their number of keyword hits, that is, the number of keywords the search engine picks up. Résumés with a higher ranking will be selected first to be passed on to a human reviewer. The more of the employer's keywords you have, the greater your chances of obtaining a high ranking and an interview.

Finding the Right Keywords

How can you know which keywords to include in your résumé? Although it is not possible to know for sure, there are ways to increase your chances. Here are some suggestions.

1. LOOK IN JOB POSTINGS. The first place to look for keywords is employ-ers' job postings for the position you are seeking. Employers purpose-fully insert keywords in their job postings to screen out those who use the shotgun approach to job seeking and automatically send out their résumé to anyone and everyone who posts an opening. Most keywords are specific *nouns* and *noun phrases* that name: (1) job titles; (2) job de-scription; and (2) job responsibilities. Noun phrases begin with strong *action verbs*. (See below.)

If you are preparing a résumé that you intend to submit to more than one employer, go through a number of job postings for the same type of position, anywhere from three to twenty postings. As you review job postings, highlight, underline, or list potential keywords that appear early in the posting as well as keywords that are repeated. You will notice that keywords vary somewhat from ad to ad. Keyword synonyms appear in some, for example. Thus, when you decide which keywords to include your resume, include some synonyms.

In your search for keywords, pay special attention to these items:

- Job title.
- A section labeled, in essence, "What we are looking for in an employee."
- Words that identify skills unique to that field or industry.
- Job description.
- Job responsibilities.
- Acronyms used commonly in that industry or field.
- Jargon or buzzwords.
- Degree requirements, including vocational certifications.
- Computer skills and knowledge, e.g. specific hardware or soft-ware programs.
- Personality traits, e.g., "self-motivated."

2. REVIEW THE EMPLOYER'S WEBSITE. Go to the website of the company you are targeting (or to websites of leading employers in your field or industry). Read the section about the firm, usually labeled "About Us." It often gives interesting details about the company's history. Be sure you understand what the company does. Look for job titles in company descriptions. Note the name of the CEO or owner, the names of divisions and where they are located. Read recent news about the company, about new products or services. Read about company profits. Find out as much as you can. Write down terminology and buzzwords that strike you as probable keywords. All this research will be especially helpful to you if you land a personal interview.

3. BROWSE CURRENT TRADE MAGAZINES AND ARTICLES. Scan for buzzwords and industry terminology currently being used. Read relevant news articles. You need to know what's happening in your field.

4. VISIT THE WEBSITES OF PROFESSIONAL ORGANIZATIONS IN YOUR FIELD. Read their publications. Attend their meetings, if possible. Read and listen for current buzzwords, especially if they are used by an officer in the organization.

5. CONSULT THE CURRENT OCCUPATIONAL OUTLOOK HANDBOOK. This is published each year by the U.S Department of Labor. Here you will find up-to-date information on job descriptions, job requirements, current employment prospects, and more. It is available online at http://www.bls.gov/oco/.

6. JOIN ONLINE CHAT GROUPS FOR YOUR FIELD OF INTEREST. Notice the current buzzwords and terminology being used in discussions. Contribute to discussion groups and blogs. Comment, share information, and ask questions. Keep current with the language being used on social media networks such as Facebook, Twitter, and LinkedIn.

7. DO AN INTERNET SEARCH. Most keywords are industry specific. You can find them used in websites and blogs that deal with your field or industry. Type in a search such as: "keywords in marketing" (or whatever field you are in). The following table gives examples of keywords listed for six different areas of interest. They are current as of this writing and subject to change (especially in the field of fashion), but they are all examples of industry-specific keywords you can find with an Internet search.

FIELD OF INTEREST	KEYWORDS
MARKETING	advance selling, agency theory, bayesian analysis, brand choice, brand management, branding, B to B marketing, category management, channel cooperation, channels of distribution, choice models, data mining, database marketing, decisions under uncertainty, diffusion of innovations, direct marketing, e-commerce, econometric models, Gibbs sampling methods, latent variable models, market entry, marketing matrixes, Markvov chain Monte Carlo methods, product positioning, targeting, time series models, word-of-mouth
ENERGY INDUSTRY	integrated company, Kyoto Protocol, climate change, green energy, environmental conservation, Exxon Valdez, OPEC (Organization of Petroleum Exporting Countries), renewable energy, nonrenewable natural resource, recycling, scarcity
FASHION	chic, on trend, fabulous, sophisticated, polished, make it work, chiconomics, eco-fashion, ethnicware, fast fashion, tribe, fashionista, prune (to express disapproval), fierce, hot, lovely, amazing, glamit, gorgeous, glamorous, ferosh (fierce, ferocious, outstanding)
ENGINEERING	ABET (accredited engineering school), AI (artificial intelligence), CAC or CADD (computer-aided design), CDSP (certified software development professional), convergence, IEEE (Institute of Electric and Electronics Engineers), IPTV (Internet protocol television), LED (light emitting diode), nanotechnology, PE (professional engineer), peer review, standards, SWEBOK (software engineering body of knowledge), Wi-Fi, WIMAX, CDMA, WSN, 3G & 4 G (The latter terms, starting with Wi-Fi, are communication technologies.)

EDUCATION	child-centered, age appropriate, balanced reading, emerging literacy, higher-order thinking, brain-based learning, authentic assessment, portfolio assessment, multiple intelligences, discovery learning, lifelong learning, hands-on, relevant, collaborative learning, block scheduling, Blue Ribbon school, education theorist, critical thinking skills
BUSINESS	strategic planning, product positioning, team-building, performance and productivity improvement, new media, organizational design, change management, competitive market, infrastructural development, investor and board relations, problem-solving and decision-making, project management, MBA, cost reduction, corporate vision, oral and written communications, customer retention, long-range planning, cost reduction

Listing Your Keywords

After you have researched keywords for your résumé, make a prioritized list of the keywords you will use. If you are unsure of which words to choose, begin by making a list of your job-related skills, since the skills an employer is looking for will be keywords. Job skills can be divided into four main groups: (1) skill in working with data and information; (2) skill in working with people; (3) skill in working with ideas; (4) skill in working with things, e.g., computers. In listing your skills and experience, be very specific. Specific words will lead you to keywords. Generalities and overused description, such as "a people person," will not be on the keyword list. Your goal is to list your job-related skills, experience, and expertise that specifically apply to the field or industry you are targeting.

Remember that keywords appearing early in job postings and repeated keywords are important, so give priority to these. Include synonyms for your terms, as well. When you have completed your list, check it against the keywords you highlighted in your first-choice job description. A general rule of thumb is that you should have *at least* 50 percent of those keywords on your list in order to get an interview. One caveat: As mentioned above, if you don't know what a keyword means, don't use it. If your résumé does lead to an interview, there is a good chance your interviewer will ask you to elaborate on some of your key buzzwords. If you can't do it, consider yourself found out.

Using Powerful Verbs

As noted above, keywords for résumés are usually specific nouns and noun phrases that apply to a field of interest or industry. Including the right keywords in your résumé is crucial to obtaining an interview. It is strong action verbs, however, that give your résumé punch. Which are more important, keyword nouns or action verbs? That is hard to say. You need to use both. Often you can't have one without the other. That is, a keyword noun phrase begins with a strong action verb.

In the sections of the résumé that describe your experience and qualifications, use short descriptive noun phrases that begin with strong action verbs. Some effective action verbs are listed in the table, below. They are shown in the past tense, since this is the tense used in résumés: e.g., "revamped recruitment strategies," "spearheaded employee recognition programs," "optimized supply chain networks."

accelerated	advanced	appraised	augmented
accentuated	advertised	approved	authorized
accomplished	advised	arbitrated	automated
achieved	advocated	arranged	awarded
acted	aided	ascertained	balanced
activated	allocated	assembled	bargained
actuated	amplified	assessed	began
adapted	analyzed	assigned	bolstered
addressed	answered	assisted	boosted
adjusted	anticipated	assumed	bought
administered	applied	attained	briefed
adopted	appointed	audited	broadened

brought	contracted	dispensed	expedited
budgeted	contributed	displayed	experimented
built	controlled	dissected	explained
calculated	convened	distributed	explored
captured	converted	diversified	expressed
cataloged	conveyed	diverted	extended
centralized	convinced	documented	extracted
certified	cooperated	drafted	fabricated
chaired	coordinated	drew	facilitated
championed	corresponded	earned	familiarized
charted	counseled	edited	fashioned
checked	created	educated	filed
clarified	critiqued	effected	finalized
classified	cultivated	elected	fixed
closed	customized	elicited	focused
coached	debated	eliminated	forecasted
coded	debugged	emphasized	formed
collaborated	decided	employed	formulated
collected	decreased	enabled	fortified
combined	defined	encouraged	fostered
commissioned	delegated	enforced	found
communicated	delivered	engineered	founded
compared	demonstrated	enhanced	fulfilled
compiled	described	enlarged	furnished
completed	designated	enlisted	furthered
composed	designed	ensured	gained
computed	detected	entered	gathered
conceived	determined	entertained	generated
conceptualized	developed	established	governed
condensed	devised	estimated	graded
conducted	diagnosed	evaluated	granted
conferred	diagrammed	examined	guided
conserved	directed	exceeded	halted
consolidated	discovered	executed	handled
constructed	discussed	exhibited	headed
consulted	dispatched	expanded	heightened

helped	issued	navigated	presented
highlighted	joined	negotiated	preserved
hired	judged	netted	presided
honed	juggled	normalized	prevented
hosted	justified	observed	printed
hypothesized	kept	obtained	prioritized
identified	keyed	opened	processed
illustrated	launched	operated	procured
imagined	learned	optimized	produced
implemented	lectured	ordered	professionalized
improved	led	organized	programmed
improvised	leveraged	originated	projected
incorporated	lifted	outdid	promoted
increased	listened	outlined	promulgated
indexed	located	outsourced	proofread
individualized	logged	overcame	propelled
influenced	maintained	overhauled	proposed
informed	managed	oversaw	prospected
initiated	manipulated	packaged	protected
innovated	manufactured	paid	proved
inspected	mapped	participated	provided
inspired	marketed	partnered	publicized
installed	masterminded	passed	published
instituted	matched	performed	purchased
instructed	maximized	persuaded	qualified
integrated	measured	photographed	questioned
interacted	mediated	piloted	raised
interpreted	mentored	pinpointed	ran
intervened	merged	pioneered	rated
interviewed	met	placed	reached
introduced	mobilized	planned	realized
invented	modeled	played	reasoned
inventoried	moderated	posted	received
investigated	modified	predicted	recommended
invited	monitored	prepared	reconciled
involved	motivated	prescribed	recorded

recruited	reversed	sponsored	transcribed
recycled	reviewed	staffed	transformed
reduced	revised	standardized	transitioned
reengineered	revitalized	started	translated
reestablished	rewrote	stimulated	transmitted
reevaluated	routed	strategized	transported
referred	saved	streamlined	traveled
registered	scheduled	strengthened	tutored
regulated	screened	structured	uncovered
rehabilitated	searched	studied	undertook
reinforced	secured	substituted	unified
reinvigorated	selected	suggested	united
related	separated	summarized	unveiled
remodeled	served	supervised	updated
rendered	serviced	supplemented	upgraded
renovated	settled	supplied	upheld
reorganized	set up	supported	used
repaired	shaped	surpassed	utilized
replaced	shared	surveyed	validated
reported	signed	sustained	verbalized
repositioned	simplified	synthesized	verified
represented	sketched	systemized	vitalized
researched	sold	targeted	volunteered
reshaped	solicited	taught	weighed
resolved	solved	teamed	widened
responded	sorted	terminated	won
restored	sourced	tested	worked
restructured	spearheaded	tightened	wrote
resupplied	specialized	totaled	
retrieved	specified	tracked	
revamped	spoke	trained	

Words *Not* to Include

Avoid résumé clichés and buzzwords that have been used so often they are meaningless. Many of them, in fact, are taken for granted as a given for any serious job candidate. There is no reason to include them. Here are the top ten words you should not include in your résumé according to LinkedIn, the professional networking website. They scanned their members' profiles (brief résumés) and found that the following ten are the most overused, overworked words and phrases posted. Here they are, listed in order, with the most overused first: (1) *extensive experience;* (2) *innovative;* (3) *motivated;* (4) *results-oriented;* (5) *dynamic;* (6) *proven track record;* (7) *team player;* (8) *fast-paced;* (9) *problem solver;* (10) *entrepreneurial.*

In addition to avoiding résumé clichés, avoid generalized, vague terms to describe your skills and experience. Instead use specific, meaningful phrases that highlight your accomplishments. Examples of generalized, vague terms to avoid include: *experienced, self-starter, goal-oriented, cutting-edge, people person, proven ability, top-flight, multitasker, proactive, perfectionist, flexible, trustworthy, fast learner, highly skilled, out-of-the-box thinker, successfully.* Contrast those generalized terms with these descriptions of specific accomplishments: *Created and implemented IT processes ... Staffed, trained, and developed restaurant managers ... Generated $1.3 million in new business in a twenty-month period ... Coordinated in-service training programs for clinical assistants.* Emphasize your accomplishments; de-emphasize your duties and responsibilities unless your aim is to show yourself as a team player. (Pardon the cliché.) Avoid such duty-driven terms as *responsible for, assisted, supported,* and *contributed.* These show you in a secondary role as a helper without specifying how you helped.

WHEN BUZZWORDS LOSE THEIR BUZZ

Stay alert. When on the job, keep your ears open. Listen to what the leaders in your field and your colleagues are saying. Any new buzzwords? If so, do you know what they mean? What new terms and lingo keep cropping up in trade journals and industry newsletters?

Evaluate new buzzwords before you decide whether or not to adopt them. The best buzzwords encapsulate the essence of a concept in a single word or phrase. They are fresh, sometimes startling, and easily remembered. They surpass their plain English synonyms in effectiveness and utility. As a result, these buzzwords enter the language and become widely used. The buzzword *social media* is a case in point. The term is unique and has no comparable synonym. It has earned its entry into our language.

But that is not the fate of most buzzwords. Most buzzwords end up losing their buzz. People hear them so often, they tune them out and find them irritating or annoying. At this point, they no longer deserve the name "buzzwords." Substitute "clichés."

If she says "at the end of the day" one more time, I'll scream!

The prevalence of this irritating state of linguistic affairs has led to the development of a Buzzword Bingo, a handmade game attendees can play on the sly when trapped in a boring meeting. Here's how it's played.

Prepare and distribute Buzzword Bingo Cards in advance of a meeting. During the meeting, players listen intently for the buzzwords on their cards and check them off one by one as they are spoken. The first player to get bingo coughs or gives a knowing nod or wink to the other players. Ironically, this very popular game, devised to avoid nodding off during boring meetings in the conference room, has an unexpected result. Instead of being lulled to sleep like their co-workers as a speaker drones on, those with Buzzword Bingo Cards sit on the edge of their chairs, fully alert, and focused with laser-like intensity on the speaker's every clichéd utterance. The speaker, unaware of what is going on, is enormously flattered by such rapt attention, which cannot but bode well for the bingo players. (It may not bode well for them, however, if someone of higher rank notices their game.)

Some have criticized Buzzword Bingo as being mean-spirited, particularly since the speaker is unaware of what is going on. Admittedly, it would be more forthright to speak frankly and advise the speaker to avoid repeating overused buzzwords. But it may not be possible to do this. In those cases, enjoy, but don't get caught!

Here's a sample card with some worn-out buzzwords.

SAMPLE BUZZWORD BINGO CARD

on the same page	leverage	disconnect	out of the box	customer-centric
game changer	reach out	value-added	It is what it is.	circle back
interface	viral marketing	FREE SPACE	at the end of the day	off line
ROI	silo	raise the bar	push the envelope	play hardball
mission-focused	touch base	low-hanging fruit	granular level	mind share

The buzzwords on the Bingo card have been around a long time. Are their meanings still clear? The sentences below show some of those buzzwords used in context. Think about how you would rephrase each of these in plain English. (See page 210 for definitions of the buzzwords shown on the Buzzword Bingo Card above.)

> We're not on the same page. We're having a disconnect. Let's discuss this later off line. I suggest we go back and silo. We need to spend time thinking out of the box. Then, mission-focused, we'll circle back and interface next Wednesday, say, after lunch—unless you want to touch base before that. At the end of the day, it is what it is!

KEEPING UP WITH THE BUZZ

Check the Internet for sites on new buzzwords in the office or in your field of interest. One such site is www.buzzwhack.com. The site is dedicated to "de-mystifying buzzwords." A recurring column is "Today's Buzz Word," which features such submissions from readers as *news snacker* (one who gets the news in short bursts from Twitter and RSS feeds), *urban Amish* (city-dweller with no cell phone, etc.), *oblication* (vacation time spent fulfilling personal obligations), and *reinventing the tire* (self-explanatory). Buzz-Whack offers some buzzword classics imprinted on T-shirts, tank tops, and mugs. Examples include: *DBT* (Death by Tweakage), *Duppie* (Depressed Urban Professional), *COTU* (Center of the Universe), *Wombat* (Waste of Money, Bandwidth, and Time), *WYSITWIRL* (What You See Is Totally Worthless in Real Life), and *YYSSW* (Yeah, Yeah, Sure, Sure, Whatever).

If you want to explore buzzwords even further, a good read is *Bizz-Words: From Ad Creep to Zero-Drag, a Guide to Today's Emerging Vocabulary* by Gregory Bergman (Adams Media, 2008). Bergman defines the new buzzwords of business, "today's essential, edgy business terms and expressions," such as *kitchen-sinked, ticker shock, capitalization, put some pants on it, frazzing, and bozo explosion.*

Other recommended books include: *Resume Buzz Words* by Erik Herman and Sarah Rocha (Adams Media, 2004); *The Buzzword Dictionary*, by John Walston (Marion Street Press, 2006); *2500 Keywords to Get You Hired*, by Jay A. Block, CPRW, and Michael Betrus, CPRW (McGraw-Hill, 2002); *Office-Speak* by D.W. Martin (Simon Spotlight Entertainment, 2005); and *Words that Sell* by Richard Bayan (McGraw-Hill, 2006).

Harnessing the power of buzzwords can get you a job, but it can also land you on the wrong side of a game of Buzzword Bingo, so listen and develop an awareness for effective communication in your workplace.

ANSWERS

CORRECT PRONOUN CASE FROM PAGE 8

(1) It is I. (2) between you and me (3) with him and me

GRAMMAR-CHECK PARAGRAPH. FROM P. <00>

If you're thinking you can rely on a spell-checker or grammar-check program **to** error-proof **your** manuscript or even to **cite** your **principal** or **everyday** errors in usage, let me **assure** you, **you're** sadly mistaken. You need to **qualify** that belief or **let** it go. Will such programs tell you, **e.g.**, **whether** to use *I* or *me* after the **preposition** *with*?

ANSWERS TO QUIZZES FROM PAGES 23–137

accept, except

(1) It's logical to expect that an Oscar-caliber actor would not **accept** a role in a ridiculously bad movie **except** under dire circumstances. (2) Thus, **except** for die-hard John Wayne fans, few movie goers could **accept** Wayne in the incongruous role of Genghis Khan in *The Conqueror*. (3) Critics did not **except** director Dick Powell from responsibility for the absurd Asian Western, whose star would **accept** an Oscar thirteen years later for his role as a one-eyed U.S. marshal in *True Grit*. (4) Evidently Powell was willing to **accept** Wayne's statement that he saw *The Conqueror* as a cowboy film and would play Khan as a gunslinger, **except** that he slung a sword. (5) **Except** for transporting the Gobi Desert to Utah, **except** for the preposterous casting of the Duke as Genghis Khan and Susan Hayward as a Tartar princess, viewers might have been willing to **accept** the premise of the film.

acute, chronic

(1) Can a virus cause **chronic** fatigue syndrome? (2) Your **chronic** lateness will get you fired! (3) She was hospitalized with **acute** appendicitis. (4) Gifted with **acute** intelligence, the chimp easily won the game of checkers from his partner, whose **chronic** hyperactivity always interfered with her ability to concentrate. (5) A broken arm is an example of a medical condition that is **acute**, whereas asthma is a condition that is **chronic**.

advice, advise

(1) Do you need an expert to **advise** you on how to solve your problem? (2) The following paragraphs give some useful **advice**. (3) Much **advice** is available on what to do when your dog has a skunk encounter—some helpful, some not. (4) The **advice** given by most dog owners is to saturate your pet in tomato juice; but others **advise** using vinegar. (5) Both pieces of **advice** simply distract the nose without curing the problem. (6) What do veterinarians **advise**? (7) Their **advice** is to mix the following in an open container: 1 quart of 3 percent hydrogen peroxide, ¼-cup baking soda, and 1 to 2 teaspoons of mild dishwashing detergent that does not contain ammonia or bleach. (8) They **advise** saturating your pet's coat with the mixture and letting it set five minutes before rinsing. (9) One last piece of **advice** is to avoid keeping the mixture in a closed container because it can explode.

affect, effect

(1) We are all familiar with the **effect** of biting into a red-hot chili pepper. (2) We may **affect** indifference, but our taste buds **effect** a protest to the fiery-hot **effect** of capsaicin, the ingredient that causes red hots to **affect** us with their built-in fire. (3) But that fiery **effect** may **affect** us in beneficial ways. (4) New studies point to capsaicin's detrimental **effect** on cancer cells. (5) For malignant cells, capsaicin can **effect** a premature death. (6) Capsaicin's fiery **effect** is put to use in a barnacle repellant applied to boats. (7) Capsaicin can **affect** and dull the perception of pain, an anesthetic **effect**. (8) The sting of capsaicin can **effect** a release of endorphins. (9) This creates the **effect** of a mild high—which explains why pepper lovers keep coming back for more, in spite of the fire.

aggravate, irritate

(1) Did Jean's remarks **irritate** John? (2) Did John's temper tantrum **aggravate** a bad situation? (3) Poison ivy can **irritate** the skin. (4) Can unusual stress **aggravate** acne? (5) Neglect of agriculture can **aggravate** poverty.

all ready, already

(1) Are you **all ready** for the big one—an event bigger than the predicted big earthquake in California? (2) This is something that **already** occurred once before, some 65 million years ago, when the Earth was **already** into the Age of Dinosaurs. (3) An asteroid collided with Earth, producing a dust cloud and resulting cold temperatures

that killed thousands of species—and, we are **already** overdue for another such colli-sion. (4) Preparations have **already** started, to ensure we will be **all ready** to prevent our extinction when the next one arrives. (5) **Already**, we are scanning the skies for approaching asteroids, and **already** we are making plans to divert them with missiles or whatever it takes. (6) Preparations are **already** being made to avoid a collision so that we will be **all ready** to defend ourselves if it becomes necessary.

all together, altogether

(1) Are you **altogether** positive that Henry is missing? (2) We did not stay **all together** as a group all the time. (3) I am **altogether** certain that Henry was with us when we left our hotel. (4) I distinctly remember us being **all together** on the dock. (5) I think we were **all together** when we boarded the ship. (6) But I am not **altogether** positive that we were. (7) We were not **all together** at the lifeboat drill, and I am sure I did not see Henry there. (8) We went to his stateroom **all together**, but it was **altogether** empty. (9) Henry is **altogether** besotted with Alexandra, but had he deliberately stayed behind to be with her—or been abducted? (10) We were **altogether** mystified as we pondered this enigma.

among, between

(1) The pharmacy is **between** the grocery store and the pet store. (2) We divided the reward money **among** the three of us. (3) Warning! **Among** the beautiful flowers in our gardens are four that can be deadly. (4) Is that foxglove **between** the two rosebushes? (5) Careful—its flowers are **among** the most poisonous if you eat them. (6) The charming autumn crocus is **among** the few flowers that bloom before they have leaves. (7) But autumn crocus flowers are poisonous and have caused several deaths **among** those who found them in the woods and tried to eat them. (8) The beautiful flowers of oleander and angel's trumpet are **among** the garden's most deadly. (9) **Among** the beauties of the garden lie some hazards, but only if you eat the flowers.

assure, ensure, insure

(1) Do you need to **insure** the contents of this package? (2) Send your letter by Priority Mail to **ensure** that it arrives by Friday. (3) Let me **assure** you that I will **insure** the vase against loss, and I will double-box it to **ensure** its safe delivery. (4) Be sure to **assure** students that our correspondence course will help **ensure**

their success in picking the right stocks. (5) Did you **insure** your house for its replacement value?

bad, badly

(1) The musicians performed **badly** at rehearsal. (2) She felt **bad** about her mistake. (3) He was **badly** scarred after a **bad** encounter with a grizzly bear. (4) Mandrake was an evil tyrant, **bad** from birth, who treated his subjects **badly.** (5) I was **badly** distressed on learning that he had paid me with a **bad** check. (6) The audience responded **badly** to the singer's outrageously **bad** rendition and pelted the stage with rotten bananas and **bad** tomatoes.

brake, break

(1) You wish an actor good luck by saying, "**Break** a leg!" (2) Don't step on the **brake** pedal when you're on a patch of ice. (3) The team got the **break** they needed to **break** their losing streak. (4) The car's **brake** fluid leaked out because of a **break** in its **brake** hose, and the **brakes** wouldn't work. (5) In a truck or train, pressurized air, not fluid, is used to put on the **brakes**.

bring, take

(1) Please **take** this letter to the post office and **bring** me a book of stamps. (2) In the 1920s, Charles Ponzi promised to **bring** investors a 100 percent return in thirty days. (3) Thousands of greedy, gullible investors were only too happy to **bring** their money to Ponzi. (4) He would, of course, consent to **take** their money, supposedly to invest. (5) In reality, he drew from that money to pay former investors, who expected him to **bring** them a return. (6) It was inevitable that the scheme would one day collapse and **bring** the authorities to Ponzi's door. (7) Ponzi's schemes were destined to first **take** him away to court, and from there, **take** him to the hoosegow. (8) Ponzi's stint in the cooler did not **bring** Ponzi lasting disgrace, for he later landed a job with Alitalia Airlines.

can, may

(1) If you're careful and **can** return it tomorrow, you **may** borrow my new digital Nikon. (2) You **may** come into my garden to look at the flowers, but beware of the beautiful foxglove flowers. (3) Foxglove flowers are poisonous and **can** kill you if you're not careful. (4) You **may** look, touch, and smell foxglove flowers. (5) But don't eat them unless you **can** withstand the stress and discomfort of a wildly racing heart, severe nausea,

and cramps. (6) On the other hand, **may** I ask if you've heard of digitalis medicine? (7) Foxglove is the source of digitalis, which **can** strengthen the heart.

capital, capitol

(1) What is the **capital** of New Jersey? (2) The state **capitol** is made of granite that was mined in the state. (3) Proposed changes to the **capital** gains tax is the topic currently under discussion on **Capitol** Hill in the nation's **capital**. (4) Does the name of a state **capitol** building begin with a **capital** letter? (5) Each state **capital** has a **capitol** building where its legislature meets.

censor, censure

(1) The **censor** deleted a seven-second segment from the TV sitcom. (2) During the war, a **censor** checked soldiers' outgoing letters for any information that might benefit the enemy. (3) It is unusual for such a prominent politician to escape criticism and **censure**. (4) According to Demosthenes, the most effective way to get rid of **censure** is to correct ourselves. (5) What did Juvenal mean when he said that **censure** acquits the raven but pursues the dove? (6) Please **censor** your remarks when children are present! (7) According to one newscaster, twenty-two percent of the people in the United States believe that the government should **censor** newspapers. (8) Do you agree with William Gilmore Simms that the dread of **censure** is the death of genius?

chord, cord

(1) Do you have a **cord** long enough go around a **cord** of wood, which is 4 by 4 by 8 feet? (2) The sonata's opening **chord** progression set a plaintive note that struck a responsive **chord** in the audience. (3) Fortunately, his spinal **cord** was not injured when a **cord** of wood fell off the truck on top of him. (4) His unfortunate demonstration of the fire hazards of overloading an electrical outlet struck a **chord** of alarm in the audience. (5) The demonstration—which consisted of plugging in a power **cord** from a space heater plus an extension **cord** to which was attached the electric **cord** to a toaster and the **cord** to a hair dryer—proved the old adage about where there's smoke, there's fire!

cite, sight, site

(1) We're standing on the **site** of the first schoolhouse in Tennessee. (2) What a **sight**, to be on the **site** at Cape Canaveral when a space shuttle is launched! (3) To **cite** the sentiments of George Bernard Shaw, "Beauty is all very well at first **sight**; but who ever looks

at it when it has been in the house three days?" (4) Can you **cite** an example of a web**site** that gives information on the senses of hearing and **sight** of the various reptiles? (5) Go to NASCAR.com, the official **site** of NASCAR, to see dramatic shots of the Bristol Motor Speedway, an amazing **sight** for the eyes, which many **cite** as the "Coliseum of Confusion." (6) To **cite** the words of racing legend Mario Andretti, "Circumstances may cause interruptions and delays, but never lose **sight** of your goal."

coarse, course

(1) Does the **course** of true love ever run smooth? (2) The film's **coarse** language was edited in order to show it on television. (3) You'll find Harry on the golf **course**, of **course**. (4) Of **course**, in the **course** of my daily skin care, I always scrub my skin with **coarse** almond granules to minimize **coarse** pores. (5) Relying on my **course** in celestial navigation, I set our ship's **course**, knowing that in due **course** we would reach Nova Scotia. (6) We will carry our canoes across this **coarse**, grainy sand to the river, then **course** swiftly downstream and arrive at our destination in due **course**.

complement, compliment

(1) May I **compliment** you on your taste in clothes? (2) This scarf is a perfect **complement** to your jacket. (3) Early in the game, cereal manufacturers learned to use the cereal box to distinguish a product from its competitors and to **complement** its contents. (4) Both celebrities and cartoon characters were paid the **compliment** of being a product's mascot. (5) Mascots were chosen to **complement** the product's perceived features. (6) For example, the choice of Norman Rockwell to paint a red-haired, freckle-faced boy for Kellogg's Corn Flakes, was a **compliment** to Rockwell's ability to project a homey, family image that would **complement** the message, "Buy Kellogg's Corn Flakes for your kids." (7) Even the box's background color, white, was chosen to **complement** the pure, clean image targeted for the product, just as yellow was chosen as a **complement** for the cheerful, energy-packed image designed for Kellogg's Corn Pops. (8) For many reasons, high sales of a boxed cereal are a **compliment** to its designer's ability to effectively **complement** the product's personality, or image.

compose, comprise

(1) Orchestras **comprise** four groups of instruments: strings, woodwinds, brass, and percussion. (2) She began to **compose** a "Dear John" letter to Harry. (3) These two

volumes **comprise** all that remains of the ancient library. (4) Eleven of the finest players **compose** the All-Star Team. (5) What five large bodies of water *compose* the Great Lakes?

continual, continuous

(1) The **continual** barking of our neighbor's dog is an annoyance. (2) There is a **continuous** stream of traffic through town during rush hour. (3) She listened to the **continuous** rush of water over the dam, punctuated by a **continual** stop-and-start buzz of a chain saw. (4) Every night, from 8:00 until 12:00, the uninterrupted, **continuous** loud music from the upstairs apartment was a source of constant irritation, which was not remedied by my **continual** complaints to the landlord. (5) The speaker droned on interminably in a **continuous** monotone in spite of **continual** attempts by the moderator to cut him off.

council, counsel

(1) When O'Reilly was in high school, he was elected to the student **council**. (2) Let's hold a **counsel** to decide how to present our plan to city **council**. (3) I am seeking your **counsel** on how to find a **counsel** for the defense. (4) Her **counsel** was that it was advisable to seek the **counsel** of an attorney who has expertise in such matters. (5) On advice of **counsel**, the **council** decided not to allocate any more funds for the questionable project. (6) Her **counsel** advised her that she should first seek **counsel** from an expert and then approach the town **council**.

desert, dessert

(1) Please don't **desert** me on this dry, arid **desert**. (2) Harvey received his just **deserts** tonight for his naughty behavior—no **dessert** after supper and no television or electronic games. (3) If you violate your orders and **desert** your military post, albeit in a sweltering, uninhabitable **desert**, the army will see that you get your just **deserts**, which will not be sweet like an after-dinner **dessert**. (4) Do I have the willpower to **desert** this luscious triple-chocolate **dessert** and leave it alone and untouched on the table?

device, devise

(1) He tried to **devise** a foolproof plan to pick the winning lottery number. (2) This state-of-the-art optical **device** will enable you to read a newspaper from across a football field. (3) Can you **devise** a **device** to open a padlock that has a combination lock? (4) During

the cold war, the proliferation of spies engendered a need to **devise** tools for spies. (5) The need to **devise** a **device** to conceal a weapon produced the fake cigarette pack, a **device** that concealed a one-shot .22-caliber pistol. (6) Another such **device** was the fake ballpoint pen that shot out teargas. (7) Since a spy may need to **devise** an escape plan, the CIA was able to successfully **devise** a unique means of escape. (8) More than a simple **device**, it was an inflatable single-engine airplane that could inflate in less than six minutes and achieve speeds up to 70 mph.

disinterested, uninterested

(1) We need impartial, **disinterested** fact finders to help resolve this controversy. (2) I find it difficult to study if I am **uninterested** in the subject matter. (3) Don't ask me about the mayoral race since I am absolutely **uninterested** in politics. (4) Far from being **uninterested**, Milbridge eats up our local politics, although you might expect him to be a **disinterested** spectator, since he hails from the British Isles. (5) Since I am **uninterested** in anything to do with math, I am **uninterested** in taking a course in statistics. (6) To render a fair decision, a judge must be **disinterested** and impartial.

e.g., i.e.

(1) The fourth president of the United States, **i.e.**, James Madison, served for two terms. (2) Some insects can sting, **e.g.**, ants, bees, wasps, and hornets. (3) Tourist attractions, **e.g.**, beaches, boardwalks, resort casinos, Revolutionary War sites, and the Pine Barrens, abound in the Garden State, **i.e.**, New Jersey. (4) Ascorbic acid, **i.e.**, Vitamin C, helps heal wounds and aids in maintaining health, **e.g.**, by resisting infection from some types of viruses and bacteria. (5) There is a vaccine available for pertussis, **i.e.**, whooping cough, which is a highly contagious disease spread through the air, **e.g.**, by coughing, sneezing, or breathing in someone's face.

elicit, illicit

(1) **Illicit** copies of the CD are being sold on the Internet. (2) His quote is sure to **elicit** outrage if we print it. (3) We must **elicit** public support to stop **illicit** sales of cigarettes to minors. (4) When his **illicit** investment scheme is exposed, it is sure to **elicit** angry responses from irate investors. (5) Once the senator's **illicit** tax-evasion scheme is exposed, it is doubtful that she will still **elicit** the support of her constituents.

emigrate, immigrate

(1) If you **emigrate** from the United States and **immigrate** to Canada, will you lose your United States' citizenship? (2) In 1849, the California Gold Rush prompted poverty-stricken laborers to **emigrate** from China and **immigrate** to the United States. (3) As long as surface gold was plentiful, the welcome mat was put out for Chinese laborers who chose to **immigrate** to California. (4) By the 1870s, gold had become scarce, the economy was in a steep decline, and laborers who been lured to **immigrate** to California became scapegoats. (5) In particular, animosity was directed toward those who had been lured to **emigrate** from China. (6) This resulted in the Chinese Exclusion Act, which barred those who tried to **emigrate** from their homeland and **immigrate** to the United States.

empathy, sympathy

(1) They were deeply moved by **sympathy** for the sufferings of the flood victims. (2) It is hard to feel **sympathy** for someone whose misfortune was caused by his own reckless behavior. (3) I feel **empathy** for those who have a fear of public speaking even though I don't suffer from that phobia. (4) The teacher has **empathy** for students who have reading comprehension difficulties. (5) He struggled to find words to express his heartfelt **sympathy**.

every day, everyday

(1) George follows the same routine **every day** when he wakes up. (2) Since the dance is not formal. You may wear your **everyday** clothes. (3) If you use this product faithfully **every day**, you will be amazed at the results. (4) Undoubtedly you have discovered that **everyday** remedies don't work. (5) You can apply lemon juice to your freckles **every day**, for example, and the only benefit will be to the lemon growers. (6) We receive glowing reports **every day** from users of Freckles Be Gone. (7) Since the sun shines **every day**, slap on some Freckles Be Gone as an **everyday** precaution before venturing outside. (8) Make Freckles Be Gone part of your **everyday** skin care program, and your skin will thank you **every day**.

every one, everyone

(1) A fad is something that sweeps **everyone** away for a brief time before it fades away and **every one** of its devotees forgets about it. (2) In 1958, when Wham-O, Inc., introduced its Hula Hoop to America, **every one** of the first twenty million was sold in six months

for $(1)98 each. (3) During the 1960s, with the Hula Hoop craze in full swing, **everyone** who had hips and the inclination was hula hooping. (4) Not **every one** of those who tried to hula hoop succeeded. (5) The hip-rotating craze was not admired by **everyone**, as evidenced by Japan's banning it on the grounds of indecency. (6) On March 3, 1939, Harvard freshman Lothrop Withington, Jr., swallowed a live goldfish on a bet for ten dollars, initiating a craze that virtually **everyone** of post-college age condemned. (7) Goldfish swallowing soon swamped college campuses and was indulged in by **everyone** game enough to try it. (8) Imagine the outrage of **everyone** who loved goldfish! (9) Fortunately, threats from the authorities slowed down the craze and soon **everyone** abandoned goldfish swallowing to take up the next craze.

farther, further

(1) Which is **farther** from Earth, Mars or Venus? (2) We'll break for lunch before discussing the problem **further**. (3) In the 1920s, astronaut Edwin Hubbell discovered that galaxies around us were moving **farther** from the Earth. (4) **Further**, by observing patterns of color in the sky and how those colors shifted in the nearer and **farther** galaxies, he was led to the conclusion that the universe was expanding uniformly. (5) In 1998, using larger telescopes, astronomers made a **further** discovery. (6) The **farther** galaxies were moving **farther** away from Earth much faster than expected. (7) Yes, the universe was expanding, but **further**, the expansion of the universe was accelerating, a phenomenon astronomers termed "the accelerating universe." (8) The **farther** ahead we look in time, the **farther** the distance between galaxies. (9) This means, **further**, that the universe will become much darker and colder in approximately a trillion times a fifty-year life span.

fewer, less

(1) Let's move to the country, where there's **less** noise and **fewer** people. (2) Because we've had **fewer** sales this year, our revenue is **less**. (3) Would you like to have **fewer** hours in a day, as the French once did? (4) In 1793, the French adopted a metric system of time keeping in which a day had ten hours, fourteen **fewer** than before. (5) Did having **fewer** hours mean that there was **less** time in each day? (6) *Au contraire*, since every hour was increased from sixty to one hundred minutes—no more, no **less**. (7) Each month had only three weeks, **fewer** weeks than before. (8) However, since each week had ten days,

each month had exactly thirty days, none **fewer**. (9) Deliberately designed to cause **less** confusion and **fewer** missed appointments, this was a most logical system, *n'est-ce pas?* (10) But the system, a triumph of French logic, was to last **less** than several decades. (11) It was abandoned by no **less** a personage than Napoleon Bonaparte, shortly after he was crowned emperor in 1804.

flaunt, flout

(1) Don't **flaunt** your engagement ring by waving it in my face. (2) They will be sorry if they **flout** my "No Trespassing" sign. (3) If you **flout** the tax laws, don't foolishly **flaunt** your mink coat and limousine—especially with an IRS. agent living next door. (4) I finally have some wealth to **flaunt**, and I'm simply following that wise old saying, "If you have it, **flaunt** it." (5) Go ahead, **flout** me and scorn my advice, but when you recklessly **flaunt** your extravagant lifestyle and **flout** conventional wisdom, you are putting yourself at risk for being reported to you-know-who! (6) I don't mean to **flaunt** my superior grasp of the language or **flout** your linguistic insensitivity, but correct usage dictates the phrase to be "reported to you-know-whom."

foreword, forward

(1) The preface of a book is written by the author, but the book's **foreword** is written by someone else. (2) We cannot move **forward** until we agree on a plan. (3) After reading the book's intriguing **foreword**, I looked **forward** to reading what the author had to say. (4) I wanted to find out for myself whether the book's **foreword** had exaggerated its appeal to **forward**-thinking readers, who envision moving **forward** to the day when humans colonize Mars.

formally, formerly

(1) He was **formerly** known as "Sweeney" before **formally** changing his name. (2) Although I have not **formally** replied to his invitation, I **formerly** indicated to him that I definitely would attend his graduation. (3) Winthorpe, **formerly** casual and careless about his appearance, was transformed after meeting the **formally** elegant Caroline. (4) His **formerly** disreputable trench coat was gone, and in its place, a **formally** cut Savile Row topcoat, the apotheosis of elegance and style.

fortuitous, fortunate

(1) The **fortuitous** circumstance of having a doctor in the house was truly **fortunate**. (2) How **fortuitous** to spot that money under the bush just when I needed it! (3) She is indeed **fortunate** to have a loving, supportive family. (4) Taking that advanced biology course turned out to be **fortuitous**. (5) This new bill is designed to provide help for the less **fortunate**.

good, well

(1) Do you think you did **well** on your algebra final? (2) Tabitha, you are a **good** cat, and such a **good** mouser! (3) There are **good** methods of fire retardation that work **well** to combat wildfires that typically ravage the Okefenokee Swamp during severe droughts. (4) Although fire retardation methods do their job **well**, however, it is not necessarily a **good** idea to use them. (5) Natural fires are **good** for the Okefenokee and are necessary to keep the swamp healthy and **well**. (6) Fires do the swamp a **good** service by keeping it **well** cleared of shrubs, small trees, and layers of peat several feet deep, whose gradual buildup would otherwise choke it. (7) The burning of peat has another **good** result in that it opens up and reveals lakes. (8) The destruction of small trees is **good** for the growth of the classic tree of the Okefenokee, the large cypress (which is fire resistant). (9) As far as wildfires in the Okefenokee are concerned, perhaps it's fair to say that all's **well** that ends **well**.

hanged, hung

(1) We washed the muddy clothes and **hung** them out to dry. (2) The outlaw was sentenced to be **hanged**. (3) When hanging pictures, use a level to make sure they are **hung** straight. (4) The famous "hanging judge," Arkansas's Isaac Parker, ordered 160 executions, of which 79 were carried out and those sentenced **hanged**. (5) The keys were **hung** on hooks attached to the closet door.

healthful, healthy

(1) Which is more **healthful**, cheesecake or fried green tomatoes? (2) If you want to be **healthy**, exercise regularly. (3) Eat a **healthful** diet in order to achieve health and stay **healthy**. (4) Here the **healthful** climate attracts those who want to feel **healthy** again. (5) These **healthful** foods are helpful foods on the road to health.

historic, historical

(1) The letter is not a **historic** document; its **historical** interest lies in the fact that it was written by Martha Washington. (2) The famous phrase "the shot heard 'round the world" is a **historical** reference to the opening shot of the Revolutionary War. (3) That **historic** shot was fired on April 19, 1775, in Lexington, Massachusetts, when the British encountered American militiamen who refused to disperse. (4) Although there is no **historical** evidence as to who fired that **historic** shot, it was followed by others, and eight Americans lay dead. (5) That **historic** event in Lexington marked the beginning of America's fight for independence.

I, me

(1) Maurice and **I** went back to Boston, where he and **I** first met. (2) Whom do you believe, him or **me**? (3) Between you and **me**, Andrea and **I** enlisted in the navy. (4) Will you feed the dog for Bernie and **me** if he and **I** decide to go to the fair? (5) Among Dean, Josh, Greg, and **me**, only Dean and **I** ordered dessert.

imply, infer

(1) What clues lead you to **infer** that Schultz has recently visited India? (2) Does that raised eyebrow **imply** you are a skeptic in regard to astrology? (3) I hope you did not **infer** from my remark that I think you should diet. (4) "Pleasingly plump" was not meant to **imply** anything of the kind. (5) Indeed, we may **infer** from numerous examples in the animal kingdom that the tendency to store fat may **imply** a superior genetic ability to survive famine. (6) You may **infer**, that I meant to **imply** that I find you pleasingly attractive. (7) I hope you will **infer** that my awkwardly stated remark was meant as a compliment.

its, it's

(1) If **it's** Tuesday, this must be Belgium. (2) Can you name this place? **Its** name comes from the Middle English word for *rabbit*. (3) **It's** been called "America's Playground" and is known worldwide for **its** hot dogs, **its** Cyclone Roller Coaster, Mermaid Parade, and Deno's Wonderwheel. (4) **It's** the one and only Coney Island. (5) **Its** reputation is well deserved.

jealous, zealous

(1) A **zealous** reporter exposed corrupt officials who had taken kickbacks. (2) Wishing to appear **zealous,** Frank made a show of taking work home every night. (3) Would you

be **jealous** if I told you I had just won the Power Ball lottery? (4) Catherine was a fervent and **zealous** reformer and was known to be a **zealous** advocate of women's rights. (5) In spite of Alvin's **zealous** attempts to get to the root of her problem, Alvina continued to feel **jealous** and insecure in their relationship. (6) Geraldine had become increasingly **zealous** in her attempts to reform Fred.

judicial, judicious

(1) Do you believe that all juries are **judicious** in rendering a verdict or in awarding large sums for damages? (2) Was it **judicious** for an Austin, Texas, jury to award $780,000 to a woman who broke her ankle tripping over her own toddler in a furniture store? (3) If lawyers would be more **judicious** in the cases they accept, our **judicial** system would not be swamped with frivolous lawsuits. (4) Lawyers were **judicious** in refusing to accept the $380 million lawsuit against Michael Jordan by a man who claimed Jordan looked like him. (5) A **judicious** provision in our **judicial** system is the ability to rule on the legality of a law (which has not, however, kept some ridiculous laws off the books). (6) In Alaska, it is unlawful to push a live moose out of a moving airplane. (A moose undoubtedly would argue that this is a **judicious** law). (7) A **judicious** use of mouthwash is recommended for garlic lovers in Indiana, where it is illegal to enter a movie theater or public streetcar within four hours of eating garlic. (8) Perhaps a **judicial** opinion should be rendered on the legality of a Pennsylvania law that requires a man to get written permission from his wife in order to buy alcohol. (9) Likewise, the Vermont law requiring citizens to take at least one bath a week—on Saturday night—should be subjected to **judicial** review. (10) Some would argue that laws to combat garlic breath or body odor are wise, **judicious** attempts to protect the sensibilities and health of citizens and to prevent public altercations.

lay, lie

(1) Did you **lay** that wet washcloth on my wooden cabinet? (2) Yes, I cannot tell a **lie**. (3) But I did not mean to let it **lie** there. (4) The Rottweiler **lay** down beside its bone. (5) I'll **lay** the towel on the sand so I can **lie** on it. (6) Before you **lie** down, **lay** the remote control on top of the television.

lead, led

(1) We need someone who will take the **lead** and **lead** us back to the cabin. (2) If we had not been **led** astray by moose tracks, we would be there by now. (3) Myles was chosen to **lead** the investigation into the mysterious death of Styles. (4) In his capacity as inspector, he had **led** many investigations in the past. (5) Did the **lead** pipe lying near the body or the dagger under the sofa **lead** him to suspect that Styles' death was no accident? (6) No, neither would have **led** Myles to pronounce that it was death by poisoning. (7) Rather, it was the faint smell of almonds in Styles' overturned glass that was the **lead** Myles needed. (8) It **led** him to suspect cyanide as the agent of death. (9) That faint odor, similar to that of peach pits, **led** to the eventual arrest of the murderer.

leave, let

(1) Please **let** me help you with that heavy package. (2) If we **leave** now, we'll beat the exit crowds. (3) The hotel won't **let** us check in until 2:00 P.M., but we may **leave** our baggage with them. (4) I hope I didn't **leave** my toothbrush at home. (5) I don't suppose you'd **let** me borrow yours? (6) Why do I always **leave** something behind? (7) The next time, I'll **let** you do the packing. (8) I'll **leave** it all to you, Mr. Perfect! (9) Now **let** me be so I can sulk for a while.

lend, loan

(1) He asked for a **loan** of ten dollars, and I was glad to **lend** it to him. (2) In the early 1920s, an investor could take out a substantial **loan** from a stockbroker to buy stock. (3) Stock prices were rising so rapidly that stockbrokers were only too happy to **lend** money secured by the value of the stock shares. (4) It was like a real-estate **loan**; investors would pay 10 percent down, and stockbrokers would **lend** them the rest—essentially, a 90 percent **loan**. (5) Isn't it risky for an investor to take out a 90 percent **loan**, and just as risky for a broker to **lend** money at only 10 percent down? (6) Because stock prices were skyrocketing, brokers felt secure in deciding to **lend** money, confident that each **loan** would be repaid—and with interest. (7) They were blissfully unaware that soon they would not have a penny to **lend**. (8) Soon they would regret every **loan** they had granted; for in October, 1929, the bubble burst and Wall Street crashed.

libel, slander

(1) The movie star sued the magazine for **libel**. (2) Can a cartoon that uses ridicule to damage the senator's reputation be considered as **libel**? (3) In anger, he uttered some

insulting, scandalous remarks that she interpreted as **slander**. (4) When you're tempted to commit **slander**, close your mouth and count to ten. (5) That contemptible lie he uttered is **slander**, and if you print it, get ready for a **libel** suit.

like, as, as if

(1) Elsa Maxwell said that nothing spoils a party **like** a genius. (2) You look **as if** you've seen a ghost. (3) That looks **like** a diamond, but is it a fake? (4) It sparkles **as** a diamond sparkles. (5) Its price is high, **as if** it were a diamond. (6) But does it cut glass **as** a diamond does? (7) Most fakes aren't hard enough because they aren't pure carbon **like** diamonds. (8) Try turning the "gem" over and looking through it **as if** it were a little window. (9) If it's transparent **like** glass, it probably is glass. (10) If you breathe on it and it fogs up for two to four seconds, **as** a mirror does, it is a fake. (11) Thus, if it looks **like** a diamond and acts **like** a diamond, it probably is a diamond.

loose, lose

(1) I hope you didn't **lose** the key to the safe. (2) The dog got **loose** because its collar was too **loose**. (3) In the 1890s the invention of the safety bicycle—comfortable, fast, and with air-filled tires—was the Victorian woman's passport to **loose** the restricting shackles of house and husband and **lose** herself in the joys of two-wheeling it, if only around town. (4) To Victorians, who were so straitlaced that a **loose** woman was one who went without corsets, the bicycle was a threat that would tempt women to **lose** their frailty, femininity, and male-dependency—perhaps even their virtue. (5) Victorian women took to bicycling like wild birds let **loose** from a cage take to flight. (6) Despite heckling, jeers, and even stoning, they did not **lose** their zest for the sport. (7) They did **lose** pounds of underwear when in 1898, the Rational Dress Society approved seven pounds as the maximum weight of a woman's underclothing. (8) Victorian fashion could not help but **lose** to the new "rational" fashion, exemplified by bloomers (gasp!) and split skirts.

may, might

(1) My homework **may** be in my locker, or a passing raven **might** have flown off with it. (2) He **might** have lived to be a hundred if only he had listened to me. (3) It **may** be that hummingbirds find red especially attractive. (4) If the game hadn't been rained out, we

might have won. (5) Since Hurricane Elva **may** arrive on Wednesday, it **may** be a good idea to buy bottled water today.

moral, morale

(1) The **morale** of an army is a deciding factor in its success. (2) What is the **moral** of the story about the race between the tortoise and the hare? (3) The group's **morale** was high because they believed they were engaged in a **moral** enterprise. (4) According to George Bernard Shaw, an Englishman thinks he is not **moral** unless he is uncomfortable. (5) During halftime, the coach boosted the team's confidence and **morale** with a spirited pep talk.

noisome, noisy

(1) At the ballgame, the **noisy** yells of the fans assaulted my ears, while the **noisome** aromas of sweat and sauerkraut offended my nose. (2) The room was so **noisy** I couldn't hear myself think. (3) The **noisome** aroma of eau de skunk dampened my enthusiasm for picnicking in the park. (4) The **noisome** fumes arising from a mixture of chlorine and ammonia produce chlorine gas and can be fatal. (5) It is so **noisy** in that nightclub that you can't hear the band, and the place reeks with the **noisome** stale smell of tobacco.

ophthalmologist, optician, optometrist

(1) Take this lens prescription to an **optician**, who will be able to make a pair of prescription sunglasses for you. (2) The **ophthalmologist** used laser surgery to repair the patient's torn retina. (3) My **ophthalmologist** called in a prescription for eyedrops that treat cataracts in the hope that I can avoid surgery. (4) An **optometrist** is not a physician but is, nevertheless, the main provider of such eye care as giving eye exams and diagnosing vision problems. (5) I'd take your eyeglasses to an **optician** to have that scratched lens replaced. (6) My local **optometrist** gave me an eye exam and offered a large assortment of frames for me to choose from. (7) The **ophthalmologist** routinely schedules operations to correct glaucoma on Wednesdays and Fridays. (8) You had better have your irritated eye checked by an **ophthalmologist** to make sure you don't have an infection from contaminated contact lens solution.

passed, past

(1) Had she driven **past** that same house sometime in the **past**? (2) A week had **passed** since he **passed** his driver's test, and he was still ticket free. (3) In the **past**, the senator

would have had no trouble having her resolution **passed**. (4) A troubling thought **passed** through Vanessa's mind. (5) Had her **past** indiscretions found her out now, after so many years had **passed**? (6) All that **past** foolishness was in the **past**, wasn't it? (7) Surely Kyle wouldn't have **passed** her letters on to Lisle? (8) That would be **past** belief! (9) She had trusted him completely in the **past**. (10) Had all his feeling for her **passed**? (11) The possibility that her **past** lover had betrayed her was too much to face. (12) Vanessa felt her knees crumple, and she **passed** out.

pediatrician, podiatrist

(1) If you suffer from corns, bunions, hammertoes, or whatever, call your friendly **podiatrist** at FootWise, where walk-ins are always welcome. (2) A **pediatrician** can tell you if little Jimmie is just teething or if he's sick. (3) Typically, a **pediatrician** begins the day with a hospital visit to see new babies and check on hospitalized children. (4) If your son had an earache or poison ivy, you would not take him to a **podiatrist** (a "foot doctor"), but to a **pediatrician**.

principal, principle

(1) What is your **principal** reason for deciding to resign? (2) The school **principal** believed that the **principle** of free speech did not give students the right to openly insult teachers. (3) What is the difference between following the **principle** of the law and following the "letter of the law"? (4) It may be the **principle** of gravity that is the **principal** cause of wrinkles and sagging skin attributed to age. (5) The irrational **principle** upon which your argument is based is my **principal** objection to it.

prone, supine

(1) She assumed a **prone** position to do push-ups. (2) I am **prone** to sleep on my back, in a **supine** position. (3) He lay down on the weight bench in a **supine** position to raise the weights above his head. (4) Harry is **prone** to be **supine**, to take the path of least effort and resistance. (5) If you lie **prone** on the floor, it may be easier to find your contact lens.

qualify, quantify

(1) How can one give a number to, or **quantify**, the impact and relevance of this research? (2) The number of years it takes for babies' names to rise and then fall in popularity helps us to **quantify** how long fads last. (3) What must I do in order to **qualify**

as a contestant on your TV game show? (4) We conducted the survey is an attempt to **quantify** the effects of our new advertising campaign. (5) It is not possible to **quantify**, or put a measure to, the value of love or of friendship or of loyalty. (6) How can I find out if I **qualify** for disability benefits from Social Security? (7) In order to **qualify** for membership in Mensa International you need only score in the top 2 percent of the population on an approved intelligence test. (8) Is an intelligence test, such as the Stanford-Binet, a reliable means to **quantify** a person's intelligence?

reign, rein

(1) She pulled back the **reins**, trying to get control of the horse, but she could not **rein** him in. (2) During the **reign** of King George III, Parliament made attempts to **rein** in the rebellious American colonists, without success. (3) In 1776, during the **reign** of Louis XVI of France, Benjamin Franklin charmed the French court and won a sizable loan for the American army. (4) The hapless King Charles II was to **reign** over England in what was arguably its worst year in history, 1666, the year of the great fire of London, in which 80 percent of the city burned down. (5) This **reign** of fire raged for five days, and even months afterwards, small fires continued to burn throughout the city. (6) Although frantic attempts to **rein** in the fire were futile, the catastrophe did succeed in putting a **rein** on the city's vast rat population. (7) So many rats and their resident fleas perished in the blaze, that it effectively put an end to the **reign** of the Black Death, or Great Plague, in that beleaguered city. (8) Afterwards, officials were kept busy trying to **rein** in citizens trying to lynch French Catholic extremists (whom they blamed for the fire, whose real cause was sparks from the oven of the King's royal baker).

set, sit

(1) Make sure all the troublemakers **sit** in the first row, where you can see them, and never let Mark **sit** next to Dennis! (2) Be very careful when you **set** down that container of nitroglycerin. (3) Please **set** your books on the counter and **sit** down. (4) If you **set** your package on the floor, someone will be able to **sit** in that seat. (5) If you **set** the television on the kitchen shelf, we'll be able to **sit** and watch it as we eat.

shall, will

(1) We **shall** go to the cabin tomorrow if you **will** meet us there. (2) No, I absolutely **will** not do what you ask, and never mention it again! (3) They **shall** follow the regula-

tions, or I'll see them in court! (4) He **will** arrive in New York at 6:30. (5) I **will** not go to Los Angeles, and there's no way you can make me. (6) I **shall** think about a trip to Las Vegas, however.

stationary, stationery

(1) Now that I've named my company, I must design **stationery** and business cards. (2) As a musician, I constantly traveled, but now I finally have a **stationary** home next to a **stationery** store. (3) I understand, however, that the **stationery** store is about to move—if a **stationery** store can move, that is. (4) During the earthquake, **stationery**, coffee cups, and pens flew off the desk, which remained **stationary**, since it was bolted to the floor. (5) Her beliefs never wavered and were as unmovable and **stationary** as the giant and noble trees she vowed to protect. (6) "Never, never will I buy **stationery** made from any but recycled paper!" she vowed.

than, then

(1) Of all the romances in history, fewer were more tempestuous **than** that of Napoleon Bonaparte and Josephine. (2) Napoleon had never been more smitten **than** when he met the beautiful Paris socialite, a widow, who was **then** thirty-two years old. (3) Josephine evaded his advances, but **then** relented, and they were married in 1796. (4) Napoleon **then** went on military campaigns. (5) Rather **than** brood over his absence, Josephine **then** attended to her own affairs, adulterous though they were. (6) On hearing about it, the enraged Napoleon **then** demanded a divorce. (7) When Josephine pleaded with him, he ended up forgiving, rather **than** divorcing, her. (8) **Then**, when he became emperor, Napoleon did divorce Josephine. (9) Hoping for a son, he married a woman much younger **than** Josephine. (10) But Napoleon had loved no woman more **than** Josephine. (11) When she died, the grief-stricken Napoleon took violets from her garden and put them in a locket, which he **then** wore until his death.

their, there, they're

(1) **There** are millions of Monopoly fans worldwide. (2) But **they're** largely unaware that **their** favorite board game helped Allied POWs escape from Nazi prison camps—thanks to the British Secret Service. (3) Operation Monopoly was **their** plan, and **they're** responsible for its success. (4) The Brits had a company making silk escape maps carried by **their** airmen. (5) The factory made Monopoly games **there**, as well. (6) Maps and

Monopoly; **they're** unlikely candidates to be paired in a secret service plot, aren't they? (7) Not to the Brits, since **their** plan was to hide escape maps and tools inside the game boxes and smuggle them into German prison camps along with Red Cross packages sent **there**. (8) They marked **their** "special edition" games with a red dot in the Free Parking space. (9) **Their** boxes were altered with carefully cut holes and slots. (10) **There** were extra playing pieces: a file, compass, and a silk escape map specific to the region and showing the safe houses. (11) **There** was real foreign currency to be used as bribes under the Monopoly˙ money. (12) To appear compliant with the Geneva Convention, the Nazis distributed Red Cross packages and the Monopoly games to **their** prisoners. (13) Of the approximately 35,000 Allied prisoners who escaped German prison camps, how many owed **their** escape to Monopoly? (14) Since security required all involved to remain silent, **their** number will remain unknown.

to, too, two

(1) Elvis Presley was no stranger **to** guns. (2) In 1970, he went **to** the White House unannounced **to** petition Richard Nixon **to** appoint him as an undercover agent **to** investigate not only drug abuse but Communist brainwashing techniques, **too**. (3) Elvis went prepared, packing **two** handguns, one for himself, the other **to** give **to** Nixon, who might need protection, **too**. (4) Not **to** be outdone, Nixon gave a gift **to** Presley—a Special Assistant badge from the Bureau of Narcotics and Dangerous Drugs. (5) The FBI got into the act, **too**, and gave Presley permits **to** carry firearms in every state **to** assist him in pursuing his undercover work. (6) Elvis kept his firearms readily available at home in Graceland, **too**. (7) He was known **to** shoot his TV set whenever Mel Torme came on the screen. (8) This treatment was accorded to Robert Goulet, **too**. (9) His car, **too**, fell victim **to** Elvis's gun-toting temper. (10) When it refused **to** start, he shot it.

vain, vein

(1) Those are **vain** promises, entirely without substance. (2) The prospectors struck a **vein** of silver. (3) In a more serious **vein**, here are the latest figures on inflation. (4) Alvin's three previous attempts to pass his driver's test were in **vain**. (5) The nurse drew blood from a **vein** in his left arm. (6) Although quite beautiful, she was not **vain** about her appearance.

was, were

(1) When you **were** in Hoboken, I **was** in Hackensack. (2) It **was** fate. (3) You and I **were** in the right place, and it **was** the right time. (4) You **were** gorgeous and I **was** rich. (5) Together we **were** perfect. (6) What **was** it the poet wrote … something about if paradise **were** now? (7) Oh, if only I **were** a poet and my words **were** poems! (8) Whether we **were** fools or dreamers—it matters not. (9) We **were** in love. (10) Or, if it **was** not love, it **was** something quite like it. (11) **Was** it to last? (12) Alas, life is not perfect; if only it **were!**

weather, whether

(1) I don't know **whether** to wash the car today or wait until the **weather** cooperates. (2) Grit your teeth and **weather** the storm, **whether** or not you're frightened. (3) No matter **whether** it rains, sleets, or snows, you know you'll have **weather**. (4) They say Los Angeles never has **weather**, but I don't know **whether** or not I agree with that. (5) It doesn't matter **whether** the **weather** is good or bad, everybody talks about it.

who, which, that

(1) Judo is not an activity **that** one usually associates with presidents. (2) Yet our twenty-sixth president, **who** was Theodore Roosevelt, was a judo enthusiast. (3) Few know **that** Theodore Roosevelt was America's first Judo Brown Belt. (4) Roosevelt practiced in the White House basement, **which** he covered with training mats. (5) He practiced with anyone **who** was available, including his wife and sister-in-law. (6) Once during a boring official lunch, he threw the visiting Swiss minister to the floor and demonstrated a judo hold, a diversion **which** delighted his guests. (7) Passing the first workers' compensation bill and pushing for stricter child-labor laws ensured the president's popularity, **which** was bolstered further when he went hunting in Mississippi and refused to shoot a black bear cub. (8) This story, **which** touched America's heart, had an interesting result. (9) People began naming their stuffed toy bears "Teddy," **which** is a name **that** has stuck.

who, whom

(1) Did you see **who** left the package at the door? (2) To **whom** is the package addressed—and **who** is the sender? (3) Ralph, **who** first noticed the suspicious package, is not one **who** is easily rattled. (4) He is, however, someone **who** easily leaps to false conclusions, and to **whom** a number of false alarms in the form of 911 calls have been attributed. (5) Perhaps this is only to be expected from one **who** devours spy novels and tales of espionage. (6) He is a person for **whom** I have the utmost respect and **whom** I hold in

deepest regard. (7) Yet Ralph is someone **who** prefers to live life as fiction, someone **who** likes to believe that behind every occurrence lurks a spy.

who's, whose

(1) **Who's** the teacher **who's** been most influential in your life? (2) It was Ms. Gillespie, **whose** words inspired me and **who's** always been a role model for me. (3) He's one of those people **whose** face is familiar but **whose** name escapes me. (4) **Who's** the author of that book about Captain Ahab, **whose** nemesis is a giant white whale? (5) **Who's** got a suggestion on a good book to read at the beach? (6) I want one **whose** plot is thrilling, a real page-turner. (7) Have you read *Who's Watching the Store?* (8) It's a spine-tingling psychological thriller by an author **who's** not only a psychologist but a forensic pathologist, and **whose** numerous honors include being awarded the coveted Edgar Allen Poe medal.

your, you're

(1) Let a smile be **your** umbrella on a rainy day. (2) Keep on smiling, for when **you're** smiling, the whole world smiles with you. (3) What is that song **you're** singing? (4) Is it, "**You're** No One If **You're** Not on Twitter"? (5) Or is it, "If **You're** Happy and You Know It, Clap **Your** Hands"? (6) I guess **you're** tone deaf. (7) Actually, I was singing, "**You're** Going to Get **Your** Fingers Burnt." (8) It's my second favorite song after "**You're** So Vain." (9) If **your** tastes run to country and western, try, "When you Leave, Walk Out Backwards So I'll Think **You're** Walking In." (10) Or, what about, "You Can't Have **Your** Kate and **Your** Edith Too"? (11) Then there's, "My John Deere Was Breaking **Your** Field, While **Your** Dear John Was Breaking My Heart." (12) Finally, here's an oldie but goodie, "You Changed **Your** Name from Brown to Jones, and Mine from Brown to Blue."

QUIZ: TRICKY SINGULARS & PLURALS FROM PAGE 161

(1) The entertainment, provided by **alumni** and **alumnae,** consisted of two **concerti** (or **concertos**) for oboe and three short **tableaux** (or **tableaus**) in which the performers took on the **personae** (or **personas**) of **cherubim** (or **cherubs**) and **seraphim** (or **seraphs**). (2) After multiple **analyses** of **data** according to agreed-on **criteria**, we were able to reject **hypotheses** whose **bases** rested on defective **schemata**. (3) If you could examine the **corpora** of the following life forms, which could contain all three of these structures— cerebral **cortices** (or **cortexes**), **testes**, and **vertebrae** (or **vertebras**): **algae**

(or **algas**), **bacteria**, **viruses**, **fungi** (or **funguses**), **hippopotamuses** (or **hippopotami**), **larvae** (or **larvas**), **octopuses** (or **octopi**), and **platypuses** (or **platypi**)? (4) After sharing **gâteaux** and **matzoth** (or **matzos**) with their former **beaux** (or **beaus**), Adele and Jeannine said their **adieus** (or **adieux**) and bravely traversed the river's raging **vortices** (or **vortexes**) to return to their respective **châteaus** (or **châteaux**) on the **vertexes** (or **vertices**) of adjoining mountains, where they contemplated their **trousseaux** (or **trousseaus**), stored in massive mahogany **bureaus** (or **bureaux**). (5) The **Burgesses**, who delighted in **minutiae**, sought to improve their **IQs** by finding errors in **encyclopedias**, recording them in **memorandums** (or **memoranda**), and submitting them to publishers' **editors-in-chief** as **errata**—or to the mediums (or **media**), if publishers made the mistake of ignoring them.

QUIZ: PROOFREADING FROM PAGE 170

Heard in a Bar

"What **ails** you, Harry? Why **sit** crying in **your beer**? **You're pale too. You're in pain**, no?" "**Aye**, George. I feel **awful**. It's really **affected** me. It's **too** hard **to bear. I erred.** I admit it. **It's all** my fault. First of all, Ellie **deserted** me—left me at the **altar, so to** speak. But **there's a lot more** to it **than** that." "Why **not** tell me **all** about it, Harry? **Let's** get down to brass **tacks.**" "**Tax!** That's just it, George. That's when it **all** started. I've **been** a **fool. I blew** it. I cheated on my income **tax. I ought** not to have done it. I lost my **sense.** Now Ellie **knows** it **too.** And now **they're** coming after me." "**Damn!** Not that, Harry! Not the IRS?" "The very same. The **Internal** Revenue Service. **There's** only **one** answer **for** me now, George. **Booze!**" "**Right** on, Harry. **I'll** drink **to** that! **But** put your **cash** away. This Bud's on me, buddy!"

DEFINITIONS OF BUZZWORDS FOR BUZZWORD BINGO FROM PAGE 185

on the same page: To be in agreement. To have a mutual understanding in regard to an issue. **leverage:** To emphasize and use to greatest advantage when attempting to do something. To use hype to fool people into thinking that what is offered is better than it really is. **disconnect:** A misunderstanding. A confusion in the communication of information. **out of the box:** Nonconformist, creative thinking. **customer-centric:** To be focused on the needs of customers. **game changer:** Someone or something that completely changes the way something is done, thought about, or made. **reach out:** To enlist the help of or involve in. To call someone and ask them to be part of your enterprise. **value-added:** Making a product seem to be a better value by making an obscure modification that in actuality adds nothing to the value of the product. **It is what it is:** An empty statement used when there is nothing to say about something or when a situation is so messed up, there's no point in trying to fix it. Another way of saying, "Get used to it." **circle back:** To revisit an issue. To come back again, welcome or not. **interface:** Brain-to-brain communication on the Internet or verbally. **viral marketing:** The technique of promoting a product or idea with a gimmick such as a free e-mail account that will cause the promotion to replicate itself and spread like a virus as customers pass it on to others. **at the end of the day:** A meaningless phrase that indicates you are about to sum up. **off line:** Out of the office. Confidential bit of gossip to be exchanged in private, out of the office. **ROI:** Acronym for Return On Investment. **silo:** To keep compartmentalized or separated. **raise the bar:** Demand a higher level of performance. **push the envelope:** To exceed previously understood expectations. **play hardball:** To be inflexible and unwilling to compromise. **mission focused:** Focused on a mission, or vision. **touch base:** To ask about a matter previously discussed. **low-hanging fruit:** Something easily accomplished or obtained. **granular level:** A high level of complicated detail; the nitty-gritty. **mindshare:** Consumer awareness of a product or brand.

INDEX

ABOUT THE AUTHOR

Nancy Ragno is co-author of the language arts series, World of Language and its predecessors, Silver Burdett & Ginn English and Silver Burdett English. She earned her M.A. at New York University and is a former teacher, lecturer, and textbook editor. In addition to her textbook series, she has written plays, biographies, and nonfiction for the middle grades and parts of numerous programs in language arts, reading, literature, speech, spelling, and social studies for major publishers. Her biography is included in Marquis' Who's Who.

Originally from Philadelphia, she currently resides in Knoxville, Tennessee, where you may often find her at Close Encounter Village in the Knoxville Zoo, where she works as a volunteer, explaining bio-facts to visitors and assisting with their "close up and personal" encounters with birds and small animals. Her interests include organic gardening, wildlife research, and playing the bassoon. During her college years, she was first-chair bassoonist of the Harrisburg Symphony Orchestra, and she maintains her interest in music and support of local musical organizations, with special emphasis on the Knoxville Symphony Orchestra.

Visit www.wordsavvy-therightword.com for more about choosing the right word.

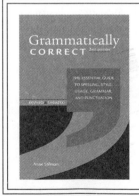